OUT OF THIS WORLD

Manchester & Merseyside

Edited by Sarah Washer

First published in Great Britain in 2015 by:

YoungWriters

Remus House
Coltsfoot Drive
Peterborough
PE2 9BF
Telephone: 01733 890066
Website: www.youngwriters.co.uk

Printed and bound in the UK by BookPrintingUK
Website: www.bookprintinguk.com

FOREWORD

Here at Young Writers our defining aim is to promote
the joys of reading and writing to children and
young adults and we are committed to nurturing the
creative talents of the next generation. By allowing
them to see their own work in print we believe their
confidence and love of creative writing will grow.

Out Of This World is our latest fantastic competition,
specifically designed to encourage the writing skills of
primary school children through the medium of poetry.
From the high quality of entries received, it is clear that
it really captured the imagination of all involved.

We are proud to present the resulting collection of
poems that we are sure will amuse and inspire.

An absorbing insight into the imagination and thoughts
of the young, we hope you will agree that this fantastic
anthology is one to delight the whole family again and again.

CONTENTS

Prenton Preparatory School, Prenton

St Anne's RC Primary School, Manchester

St John's CE Junior School, Manchester

St Luke's CE Primary School, Oldham

Grace Todd (10)...................................... 84
Laaibah Imran (10) 85
Emily Kerwin-Royle (9).......................... 85
Lilia Mercado (10).................................. 86
Amber Faulkner (9)................................ 86
Demi Darlington (10) 86
Lilia Smith (9).. 87
Charlie White (9)................................... 87
Luis Mercado (10).................................. 87
Maria Ahmed (9).................................... 87

St Margaret's Anfield CE Primary School, Liverpool

Grace Kettle (9) 88
Kostas Kuklys (9)................................... 88
Bradley Wasley (8) 89
Ella Dooley 89
Francis McCabe-Madden (9)................... 90
Libby Barr (9).. 90
Jocelyn Culshaw (8) 91
Ben Blackham (8) 91
Emily Richardson (9) 92
Ella Jones (9).. 92
Aaron Hampson (8) 93
Kaylyn Grace Dawe (8) 93
Laurie Stowers (8) 94
Abbi-Lynn McGovern (9) 94
Ruby Belle Davies (8)............................. 95
Leah Power (9) 95
John-James Evans (9)............................. 96
Tassyana Silveria-RSmith (8) 96
Holly Mason (9) 97
Jack Anthony Robinson (9)...................... 97
Daniel Porter (8) 98
Brogan Courtney Towner (9) 98
Gabrielle Thomas (8).............................. 98
Rida Fatima (8)...................................... 99
Daniel McDermott (9) 99
Sydnie Foster (8)................................... 99
Frea Rose Beth Johnston (8) 100
Katie Millington (9)............................... 100

St Mary's CE Primary School, Manchester

Jorja Grace Lily Miller (10)................... 100
Caitlin Jones (9)................................... 101
Faith Megan Robinson (10)................... 102
Rachel Phillips (9)................................ 103
Kiera Massey (9) 104
William Guy Nixon (10).......................... 105
Mille Hooper (11) 105
Matthew James Rupert
Dickinson (10)...................................... 106
Lucy Barrett (10).................................. 106
Phoebe Tootell (11).............................. 107
Casey Myers (10).................................. 107
Daisy Grace Goddard (9) 107
Phoebe Caine (9) 108
William Henry Marshall (11).................. 108
Thomas Matthew Jarman (9)................. 108

St Patrick's RC Primary School, Manchester

Samuel Adeoye (9)............................... 109
Zoe Price 110
Niat Kahsay (8).....................................110
Sonny Drake (9) 111
Darren Njomo (9)..................................111
Yaruuna Lkhagvajav (8)........................112

Sedgley Park Community Primary School, Manchester

Kacper Hagedorn (10)...........................112
Samir Hussain 113
Hasan Gohar (11)..................................113
Haneeah Warda Fazel (10) 114
George Eze (11) 114
Adeel Malik (10)....................................115
Zainab Patel (10)..................................115
Emaan Mohammad (10).........................116
Weronika Okwieka (10) 116
Danyal Uddin (10).................................117
Antoni Magon (10).................................117

Temple Primary School, Manchester

The Heys Primary School, Ashton-Under-Lyne

West Kirby Primary School, Wirral

Westvale Primary School, Liverpool

THE POEMS

It's All Over

The wind rolled in a blanket of darkness,
As the stormy seas rose,
The trees blazed a thunder,
As he walked upon the solitary road,
The night seemed to disappear,
As he was somewhere near,
The fate he would endure,
And the soldier went marching – marching – marching,
To 'no-man's-land',
A never-ending fate.

He has a green tin helmet on his forehead,
An itchy chin,
A coat of linen,
And blots of pale white skin
They were much too big,
His boots infested with nits,
The mud was like a fixture of death,
At least his sniper would be able to blast again.

The mud slowly dissolved into his feet,
I am doomed,
Cursed,
I will soon be no more,
I wish the earth around me would fall,
A bullet would hit my heart,
All for the love of my maiden,
For my maiden,
The one I love.

Hazel Sibanda (9)
Armitage CE Primary School, Manchester

What D'ya Wanna Be?

Yo, yo, yo, this is your boy Joe
Sitting in my house with all my bros,
I need to ask a question, what do you wanna be?
Don't take your time just tell me.
Maybe a singer and go to the Voice
Or a footballer, go join Marco Reus
I'm just sitting here making things rhyme
Oh! be a policeman, go fight crime.
Maybe be the best and beat the rest
Or an egg head, do well in your tests
Maybe a movie star, you're on TV
When you're finished you have a cup tea, break it down,
Or a lawyer, a baker, a faker, a maker, a slender, a gamer,
A dancer, a mender, a breaker, a wrecker, or a teacher.
I'm singing this song cause my friends once told me, what d'ya
wanna be?

Joseph Coughlin (10)
Armitage CE Primary School, Manchester

What Do You Want To Be?

You could be the most hilarious,
You could be the best,
You can have something written all over your chest,
You could see the world,
Visit Paris or change your name to Harris.
What do you wanna do?
You could be famous or just flawless!
Maybe an imperceptive wallflower is more you thing
Or blasting into space while your heart palpitates
Or maybe being the artist you can be!
Maybe you want to meet the queen and be ostentatious,
Or be a lawyer who begs to differ while being suspicious
Whatever, whatever, just decide what so you wanna be?
Hold up your pride.

Afranur Tabassum (11)
Armitage CE Primary School, Manchester

What D'ya Wanna Be?

Hey you, what d'ya wanna be?
Maybe you wanna be an actress and be an entertainer on TV
Or be police, fighting crime, cracking the cases,
You can be a model, the best of all,
Looking like Beyonce working that stuff, working that style!
You can be like Ariana Grande singing out loud
You could be a designer and be a creator making all the clothes in the world!
Maybe you could be a lawyer, the smartest in the courtroom, solving them cases
Or you could be faster than Usain Bolt, you'll be sprinting all day
Or you could be like Messi showing off them skills,
Having the most football fans looking up to you!
You could be chef and make the best food and open up the most famous restaurant!

Vivienne Gomez (11)
Armitage CE Primary School, Manchester

What Do You Want To Be?

Hey you, what d'ya want to be?
Hey kid, you don't have to tell me.
I am just here to read some poetry, what d'ya want to be?
Want to be a teacher that teaches all sorts of things
Or a preacher that speaks to the lord, you see
Maybe you wanna be a baker
Or maybe a faker that acts all the time, you see.
Maybe a fool or a cool person, you see.
Maybe a ballerina or a basket ball player
Or maybe an astronaut that explores Uranus
Or maybe a king that owns some rings.
They say, 'Yeh, yeh, yeh,' and see some real bling.
If you want!

Ebony Knight (11)
Armitage CE Primary School, Manchester

What D'ya Wanna Be?

Hey you stop there, I wanna read you some poetry called, what do ya wanna be.
Do you wanna be the first person on Mars or a gladiator who fights in war.
Or maybe you just like going with the flow, do whatever it's you choice.
Be a star you could go far, don't listen to negative praise cause you'll be okay.
What do you wanna be?
I'll say it again, be a baker not a faker or someone who's a lifesaver.
Just be who you are and you'll go far.
It's your mission, your mission alone to decide what you wanna do or what ya wanna be.

Elfina Hancock (11)
Armitage CE Primary School, Manchester

What D'ya Wanna Be?

Hey you, what d'ya wanna be?
Footballer, goalkeeper, referee.
You must decide, it's not on me,
Cause I could just be home with my family.
Do you wanna have the brains to multiply
Or be like Superman and have powers to fly?
These things can happen to any random guy
But to be successful you can't be shy.
Do you wanna be a wrestler and deliver a slam
Or be a good cook and cook up some lamb?
You don't have to listen, it's your decision,
But if you do you're gonna have to keep up to my cool rhythm.

Joel Mason (10)
Armitage CE Primary School, Manchester

What D'ya Wanna Be?

What d'ya wanna be?
Do you wanna be a famous footballer and act all tall?
Maybe you wanna be a legendary football player and shake hands with the mayor
Look it's not up to me but may I suggest that you put it in po-et-ry.
What d'ya wanna be?
Do you want to be a well-achieving surgeon just like me?
It's better if you decide coz it's not my future to see.
Everything's up to you but what I'm saying it's all true.
What d'ya wanna be?
Do you wanna be racing Hamilton in the brand new Grand Prix?
No matter what I say it's your pick coz it's your future to be.

Kai Reid (11)
Armitage CE Primary School, Manchester

What Do You Wanna Be?

What do you wanna be, a superstar?
With loads of money and visit Jupiter.
You can be a dancer, winning all the competitions as you go.
Maybe you wanna be a maker, a baker, a slender or even a lifesaver.
You might even wanna be on TV shows,
Breaking all the records that could have never been broke.
You might even be an artist making plenty of money as you go.
You might even be on Britain's Got Talent.

Anita Imagbe (11)
Armitage CE Primary School, Manchester

Ten Things Found In An Astronaut's Pocket

1. A bucket full of shiny silver moon dust,
2. Part of Saturn's huge silky ring,
3. A UFO as mini as a mouse,
4. Asteroids raining down on the bottom of the box they are kept in,
5. The silence is deadly inside the container,
6. An alien puppy just for you,
7. A tub of showering stars,
8. Neptune as cold, dark, windy and mysterious as ever,
9. Jupiter as bold as brass,
10. A black hole contained for now.

Aeryn Hindle (9)
Fiddlers Lane Community Primary School, Manchester

Ten Things Found In An Astronaut's Pocket

1. A handful of glistening shooting stars,
2. Pluto a faraway dwarf star,
3. Colourful planets all of them beautiful
4. A shimmering moon in the starry night,
5. The sun as bright as a raging fire,
6. Neptune originally 8th from the Sun now the furthest,
7. Asteroids just past Mars and just before Jupiter,
8. The Sun – all the planets orbit around it,
9. A comet it's just like a shooting star,
10. Earth – 3rd from the Sun, it's made almost of all water.

Callum Rocliffe (9)
Fiddlers Lane Community Primary School, Manchester

Ten Things Found In An Astronaut's Pocket

1. A handful of gleaming shooting stars,
2. The Milky Way as white as outspread milk,
3. Scarlet Jupiter, spinning through the silent universe,
4. The marvellous Moon spinning in its orbit round the super Earth,
5. Mars as grey as an Elephant,
6. Asteroids zooming through the silent stars,
7. Neptune as cold as the arctic,
8. Uranus as blue as the ocean,
9. The eerie silence of the solar system,
10. Sun, the huge planet in the solar system.

Lucy Rowbotham (9)
Fiddlers Lane Community Primary School, Manchester

Ten Things Found In An Astronaut's Pocket

1. The Milky Way as white as spilt milk,
2. The whistling of a shooting star,
3. Rusty red Mars spinning behind Earth,
4. The sky as black as ink,
5. Jupiter as big as an elephant,
6. Whooshing of an asteroid,
7. The moon as light as a feather,
8. Neptune as light as baby blue,
9. Exploding of a shooting star when hitting the moon,
10. Super Saturn orbiting next to giant Jupiter.

George Monks (9)
Fiddlers Lane Community Primary School, Manchester

Ten Things Found In An Astronaut's Pocket

1. Mars as red as a London bus,
2. A giant meteor zooming through the evening sky,
3. A huge shiny satellite,
4. A boiling hot Mercury
5. A Milky Way as white as a glass of milk,
6. A massive sun heating him up,
7. Spaceships as massive as a universe,
8. An Earth as blue as sky,
9. The universe as black as coal,
10. Saturn as yellow as a banana.

Leon Walker (10)
Fiddlers Lane Community Primary School, Manchester

Ten Things Found In An Astronaut's Pocket

1. The shooting rockets in the ebony sky,
2. Saturn's rings rolling around,
3. A blinding sun next to Mercury,
4. The Earth as blue as water,
5. The moon as white as snow,
6. Mars, the dry rocky red planet,
7. shocking stars as bright as a search light,
8. Jupiter as red as blood,
9. Neptune the coldest planet like the antarctic,
10. Space that has been there for infinity.

Sam Skeels (10)
Fiddlers Lane Community Primary School, Manchester

Ten Things Found In An Astronaut's Pocket

1. A pocketful of luminous shooting stars,
2. Jet black space full of colourful planets,
3. Mars as hot and rusty as fire,
4. Jupiter as huge as a giant,
5. Asteroids shooting, crashing in the sky,
6. Indigo Neptune furthest from the sun,
7. Space as silent as a church mouse,
8. Spinning Earth orbiting the sun,
9. The Milky Way as white as milk,
10. Spherical planets spinning round and round.

Chloe Louise McCarthney (9)
Fiddlers Lane Community Primary School, Manchester

Ten Things Found In An Astronaut's Pocket

1. The roar of a marvellous meteor crashing down,
2. The Sun, the brightest light ever!
3. Super, spherical planets orbiting the Sun,
4. Glistening, shooting stars zooming past,
5. The Moon, as round as a ball,
6. Indigo night sky, with all the planets in order,
7. A diamond-white rocket about to blast off,
8. Whispering stars, twinkling all around,
9. In space, luminous colours everywhere you look,
10. Deadly silence!

Sophia Langtree (9)
Fiddlers Lane Community Primary School, Manchester

Ten Things Found In An Astronaut's Pocket

1. A pocketful of whispering stars,
2. The Moon as round as a ball,
3. Spherical Sun burning in the universe,
4. Satellites exploring the beautiful planets,
5. The rusty red Jupiter as large as a basketball,
6. All the amazing planets orbiting the stunning Sun,
7. Exploding stars bursting into black holes,
8. The colourful galaxy, like a pack of Smarties!
9. Mercury as small as a bouncy ball,
10. The crescent Moon reflecting off the gleaming sun.

Paige Collier-Hindley (10)
Fiddlers Lane Community Primary School, Manchester

Ten Things Found In An Astronaut's Pocket

1. The shining, rusty planet Mars,
2. Amazing jet-black space with wonderful planets,
3. Fantastic shooting stars so bright as light,
4. Milky Way so bright as snow,
5. Jupiter, the largest planet in the solar system,
6. Stunning space with planets that orbit the Sun,
7. The Sun as bright as galaxies,
8. The bright stars in the night sky twinkling,
9. Meteors flying by second after second,
10. Galaxies that lead to the Milky Way.

Tom McMillan (9)
Fiddlers Lane Community Primary School, Manchester

Ten Things Found In An Astronaut's Pocket

1. A gloomy ebony sky full of shooting rapid stars,
2. Mars, as red as blood in its orbit,
3. The Sun, as bright as a burning diamond,
4. Mercury, battering through its orbit,
5. Jupiter, as big as a giant spinning around the stars,
6. Saturn, as spherical as a ball floating in the sky,
7. A twinkling star, glowing the universe,
8. Neptune, as blue as the shining sky,
9. Pluto, as small as a pea on a plate,
10. Milky Way, as white as a piece of paper.

Connor Sykes (9)
Fiddlers Lane Community Primary School, Manchester

Ten Things Found In An Astronaut's Pocket

1. A handful of gleaming shooting stars,
2. Spherical Uranus in a peaceful silence,
3. Mars as red as blood, spinning around the Sun,
4. An indigo rocket about to blast off,
5. Crescent Moon hanging from a jet-black sky,
6. Jupiter, the orange and white giant in the universe,
7. Navy Neptune the brilliant last planet from the Sun,
8. Luminous yellow Sun shining brightly on Venus,
9. Pluto, the amazing dwarf planet just fits inside the solar system,
10. Milky Way, as wide as a massive hole through space.

Katie Davies (10)
Fiddlers Lane Community Primary School, Manchester

Ten Things Found In An Astronaut's Pocket

1. Ebony sky full with bright, twinkling shooting stars,
2. Asteroids crashing as loud as an explosion,
3. Stunning solar system spinning around my pocket,
4. A bucket full of deadly darkness,
5. A handful of twinkling stars,
6. The grey Moon is a ball,
7. A scarlet red fiery ball in my pocket,
8. Whoosh of a colourful rocket going out of the solar system,
9. The galaxy spinning around as Saturn is orbiting the stunning Sun,
10. The whispering of the stars.

Kacey Retford (9)
Fiddlers Lane Community Primary School, Manchester

Ten Things Found In An Astronaut's Pocket

1. A pocketful of glistening spherical planets,
2. A candy moon as large as a basketball,
3. A colourful rocket blasting into the universe,
4. Venus redder than a bunch of roses,
5. Three electric blue asteroids,
6. Exploding stars turning into black holes,
7. Uranus, cold as a block of ice,
8. A handful of whispering stars
9. An elephant bigger than Jupiter,
10. Space as quiet as a mouse.

Harleigh Chappel (9)
Fiddlers Lane Community Primary School, Manchester

Ten Things Found In An Astronaut's Pocket

1. A luminous gloomy green Milky Way,
2. A sun is a light shining in the pocket,
3. Astonishing asteroids crashing around,
4. The dark night as black as ebony wood,
5. Marvellous Mercury whizzing around the stunning sun,
6. Whoosh of a stunning star,
7. The Sun wriggling around,
8. A glimmering galaxy glooming around,
9. A diamond rocket taking off,
10. Mars spinning around with its scarlet colour.

Lia Marie Sykes (9)
Fiddlers Lane Community Primary School, Manchester

My Beautiful Dream

One day when I slept I had a beautiful dream,
I was in a fairy land having mountains of ice cream.
There were little dwarves skiing in the mountains,
Sliding up and down over the creamy fountains.
I reached one of the dwarves and asked about the Fairy Queen,
He pointed to the castle opposite a milky stream.
I flew to the castle fluttering my pink wings,
And met the Fairy Queen dressed in silky sheen.
She took me all over the castle and specially to her toy den,
Where we played together with all her little friends.
I wish it was all real but it was a dream,
I realised this as my mom woke me up from my sleep.

Bhavya Belwal (7)
Holy Cross Catholic Primary School, Liverpool

My Day

I was running down the road so fast,
I see my best friend pass,
He came up to me and said 'what do you want?'
I told him that I had just come for a jog,
My legs were so sore I didn't know what to do,
So I went and told my mum and she made me a brew,
I watched TV and played on my game,
And my sister came in who was in pain,
She was crying so loud that I covered my ears,
Then my dad came running up saying cheers,
He noticed that I was just sitting down,
So he got me up and spun me around,
The lights started flashing,
And the music began,
I started to dance,
But then I heard a bang,
I looked outside to see my cat,
Chasing a rat,
I laughed so hard,
That it made me fart,
Everyone was giggling,
And I was shivering,
The time went on,
And everyone had gone,
So I had to start my homework,
But I sang,
Homework, oh homework,
I hate you, you stink,
I wish I could wash you away in the sink.

Kyle Miello (8)
Holy Cross Catholic Primary School, Liverpool

On Holiday

I love going on holiday.
I love going to a different place.
I love going swimming there.
I love playing in the clubs.
I love going to a hotel.
I love making friends there.
I love going out.
I love getting a car.
I love going around the cities.
I love spotting different parks.
I love playing with my sister.
I love going on holiday.

Rawan Zadeh (8)
Holy Cross Catholic Primary School, Liverpool

The Mermaid

Look there's a mermaid!
She has a long braid.
Just like me.
She is as beautiful as a unicorn.

She smells like popcorn.
Her tail is splashing in the water.
She is sitting on a rock full of weeds.
She is looking at the humans.

Her eyes are gleaming green.
I'm scared if she sees me.
So I have a last look and walk away.

Samiksha Gupta (8)
Holy Cross Catholic Primary School, Liverpool

Solar System

S un is the hottest star
O ur planet is the Earth
L ots of planets are in the solar system
A steroids and comets too
R ound the orbits the planets go

S hooting stars travel very fast
Y ou should make a wish if you see one
S tars and moon only come out at night
T hey are shy during daytime
E arth is the only planet that has gravity
M ilky Way galaxy is where you find the solar system.

Jason Do (7)
Holy Cross Catholic Primary School, Liverpool

Kitten

Dedicated to Mindy

Sapphire eyes shone so bright
Sharp teeth gleaming white
Twitchy pink nose cute as a button
She paused from feasting on her mutton

Pattering softly off to bed
She smoothed out her pillow and rested her head
Playfully licking her creamy peach fur
She let out an alarming purr

When she awoke, she gave a yawn
Underneath her I could see the pillow was torn
I peeked inside and couldn't belive my eyes
There were about six kittens, every colour, every size

I stared at them in shock, utterly amazed
Their mother licked her paw, not at all fazed
I picked up a small one, white as snow
Her diamond eyes glittered and began to glow.

Nicole Berger (11)
King David Primary School, Manchester

Parking

My mother was getting frustrated.
Her face was turning red.
You could tell she wasn't elated.
She turned around and said;
'Why aren't there any spaces?'
Suddenly she cheered, she'd found a space.
We clambered out of the car,
And walked to the shopping centre.

I ran into the sports store,
And grabbed football boots, socks and more.
My mum led me to the till,
And stared hard at the bill,
But when she looked at my pleading face,
She picked up the boots by the lace,
And put them in a plastic bag.

We went into a shop, where the smell made me gag.
There were perfumes of all sizes and shapes,
They smelled of strawberries, oranges or grapes.
My mum had a bag filled with cosmetics.
How I wished instead, they were electrics -
An ipad mini, a music player.
As I was daydreaming, my mum yelled 'Freya!'
I leapt to my feet,
We went to the car and put the bags on the seat.
When we tried to drive home, a car blocked our way!
My mother was getting frustrated,
Her facing was turning red.
You could tell she wasn't elated.
I gazed at the window, sighed and shook my head.

Freya Demby (11)
King David Primary School, Manchester

The Storm

As I came people ran,
The nearer I got the more they ran,
Ran to the rabbit burrow shelters,
Country to country, I go,
The same reaction,
Terror shows.

I want to be friends,
I want to see them be happy,
Happy to see me,
And not flee in terror,
Why do they hate me?
I want to know,
They don't hide it,
They let it show,
They hate me!
I cry,
They hate me!

Sometimes I get mad,
Then I cause catastrophes,
Wrecking, demolishing,
And a whole lot more.

When the storm comes,
Remember to greet it before it gets mad,
Become friends with the storm.

When the storm comes in,
Remember to greet me before I get mad.

Sophie Jayson (10)
King David Primary School, Manchester

The Terrible Teacher

Ding, it's the end of school,
Mrs Crow's pupils can't flee fast enough!
Young Alice can't leave her class without sobbing,
She's the terrible teacher.

Her ill-flavoured, wrinkled face,
Caked with a boatload of makeup.
She's a monster, she is, students say:
She's the terrible teacher.

Her mouth is like a dripping cave,
When she yells at me.
Her circular spectacles sit at the end of her nose,
She's the terrible teacher.

A mole persists on her top lip,
Where a thin moustache almost lies.
When she rarely smiles, her gap-toothed gob shows,
She's the terrible teacher.

The old woman can barely teach,
She sits and stares all day.
Expecting us to produce some work,
She's the terrible teacher.

Mrs Crow, be aware of her,
She's vicious,
She's cruel,
She's out of her mind.
She's the terrible teacher . . .

Tali Levene (11)
King David Primary School, Manchester

Mars

Beyond the rusty desert dunes
And the rocky, ruby mountains,
Is there more than dust
Or an eternity of vast emptiness?
No life lies
In the stormy rubble,
A pile of red -
Yet gloomy and black
In the never-ending blackness.

With flickering stars
Looming over nothingness,
Struggling to penetrate
The gloom;
And failing,
Is it the ever-greater emptiness
Or the blackness that creates the misery?
Or is it the red blotch beyond the craters of the Moon?

An icy cold gnashes and bares it dagger-edged teeth,
A cold that grasps and grapples
The blood-red,
The colour of danger
That watches like a bloodshot eye.

So much to discover beyond the mystical rings of Saturn,
And the hurtling, blazing comets.
But will we look on, and only see Mars?

Abigail Hurst (11)
King David Primary School, Manchester

The Alphabet Of Unpleasantness

A is for apples with worms inside
B is for bad breath but nowhere to hide
C is for cake that you're not allowed
D is for dogs that bite your mouth
E is for essay that you have to do
F is for failing the essay in school
G is for girls that quarrel all day
H is for house bills you forget to pay
I is for ice rinks that you fall on
J is for jobs that are good but a con
K is for kites that get stuck in the tree
L is for boring literacy
M is for movies that are pure rubbish
N is for newspaper that's badly published
O is for only one on your own
P is for when you really want a phone
Q is for quarrels between you and siblings
R is for phone when it goes *ring*, *ring*
S is for stepping in something icky
T is for time when it's ticking
U is for umbrellas that don't work in the rain
V is for vicious pets, ow the pain!
W is for weather when it's bad
X is for xylophone it's broken, I'm sad
Y is for yoghurt that looks like slime
Z is for zero out of ten on this rhyme!

Libby Bennett (11)
King David Primary School, Manchester

A Snake

Snake, it is,
A bearing thing to be seen
Though despite its daring stare:
It's a delicate diamond in heaven,
It slithers like a stream
Towards its home to protect
It's pattern shining, as bright as gold,
Underneath its hate.

Tis there indeed – yet gaze again
As it shows off its daring scene
Quickly and viciously bites into flesh,
Blood rushes out, the animal screams
It runs away while limping from its wound,
A cycle it is, one that snakes all know.

Will it die, will it live?
A question we might never know
But its spirit could rise -
Rise to the heavens,
But even then we shall not know
The nature of snakes
One that humans will never guess,
For they are blind – blind to the species of snakes.

Ellouise Maya Pinnick (10)
King David Primary School, Manchester

Way Up High...

I gaze up at the silent, starry sky,
Oblivious to what is happening right before my eyes,
A million comets zooming across the sky,
Not a single one will be seen again for years and years and years.
The silent valley up above,
In space no one hears you scream,
Twinkling wonders, appearing every night,
Floating satellites controlling our tech,
But on earth they are a tiny speck,
A freezing chill down your spine.
Astronauts floating,
The rockets flare blasts it up, up and away
A stretching machine way up high,
Men growing taller from the sky.
Tiny specks blocked around, twinkling all the time,
This all actually happens way up high!

Jack Moss (10)
King David Primary School, Manchester

The Interview

Here I am outside the door
Waiting for that awful call,
My hands are shaking,
I can't bear the waiting,
Plus I'm on the edge of fainting

I walk in the room
And the boss says 'Mr. Loom!'
He asked me questions
That he forgot to mention
And after, there was a lot of tension

It's finally done
Can't wait to tell my mum,
It went so well!
Who should I tell?
Ooh, how about my sister, Mel?

I got the job,
I'm so pleased,
And now I'm on my way to Leeds.

Sonny Waxman (11)
King David Primary School, Manchester

My Imaginary Friend

No one made a friend-guide kit,
So why not bend the rules a bit?
My friend's cooler than anyone else
And doesn't only care about himself.
People tease and say he's not real,
But that's not the way I feel.
Even though my friend is not in sight,
I think they are jealous because we don't fight
That's not the person I want to be,
Doesn't matter if everyone can't see him
Because he's real to me.

Libbi Rubens (11)
King David Primary School, Manchester

School Lunches

Queuing up in the school canteen,
Waiting for our lunch,
It's the worst sight I've ever seen,
Watching the children go *munch*!

It's unusual, they like it,
I think it's slop,
Obviously I have to eat a bit,
But I don't like it a lot.

I normally devour meals,
All in one,
In school it's completely unreal,
How it's the opposite of fun.

So let me warn you,
Don't eat school food,
It tastes like mushy goo,
And you'll be in a rather angry mood!

Lauren Isaacson (11)
King David Primary School, Manchester

Hands

Some people don't think,
Some people ignore,
They don't even acknowledge
About what hands are for.

You pick up your pen,
Then you write down a letter,
Your hands are controlling it
Better and better.

Your hands can move,
And create and paint,
They can greet Uncle Bob
And wave at Aunt Kate.

Sadie Shapiro (10)
King David Primary School, Manchester

Betrayal

Sat alone, in the corner of the playground,
Head on my knees, shaking all over.
Tears slowly falling, dampening the earth,
The tears of a betrayed soul – unwanted, forgotten.

Why do they always forget me,
Leave me out, hate me?
Do I have a real friend,
Within this cruel, cruel world?
Is life worth the heartache and pain
That you feel more than anything
When being betrayed?

I've fallen into a hole
That I cannot climb out of.
A hole of woe,
Despair,
Betrayal.

Ella Vardi (11)
King David Primary School, Manchester

Brave It!

I stepped up on the diving board,
My feet step one after another to the end of the platform,
As I look down at the water,
My mind starts to say 'Don't do this!'
But I say to myself 'Yes I can',
I was about to jump but my mind says 'No',
So I thought 'Let's do this!'
I jumped off the board in fear,
Slowly I touch the ground
Then I say 'Let's do it again'.

Ollie Goodman (10)
King David Primary School, Manchester

The Horrible Days At School

Today I have to go to school,
I really think that's kind of cruel.
The boring lessons and nothing being learnt.
Especially the horrible. disgusting lunch,
That the evil dinner ladies make us munch.
The horrible days at school.

The awful food that we've got to eat,
Or the disgusting pasta or even meat.
The lunch ladies' slobber dripping on the food,
Which makes everybody sick and in a bad mood.
The horrible days at school.

And worst of all the teachers smell,
When I walk into the hall especially Mrs. Mell.
They smell of fish or even pie,
Not one person even says hi.
The horrible days at school.

Louie Lerman
King David Primary School, Manchester

Snowflakes

They fly around in the calm, placid breeze,
Swirling and bouncing as you sneeze
From the cold winter weather.
Children shiver whilst flakes fall in their hair,
As they fall to the ground the children stare.
On the trees the buds are covered in ice,
They fall on the buds like cats chasing mice.
Every winter when the sun awakes,
They arrive most of the time
They are called snowflakes.

Ruby Chaytow (11)
King David Primary School, Manchester

The Tea Party

There's a big chocolate fountain sitting neatly on the table,
So much food my stomach's unable!
Gold lined ceramic jugs, saucers and spoons,
I can see my reflection in the full silver moon.
Three tiers, four tiers, five tiers or more.
Thousands and thousands of crumbs on the floor.
I suddenly see it standing there.
A giant blood crimson gummy bear!
Oh wait, a lone lost salad on the ground,
Suddenly the whole world doesn't make a sound.
Is this a message that I should go,
For the healthier option, Oh no!
Maybe I should eat it and turn a new leaf.
It's a better choice for my body and my teeth.
Maybe a salad party from now on,
All the bad food, going, going, gone!

Gabrielle Kaufman (10)
King David Primary School, Manchester

Lunchtime

The worst time of the day
The time it is to play
Old meat loaf served on your tray
The fatness inside
Old fingernails fried,
Right now if I'm being honest, I think something died.
The handmade chocolate cake
Oh, where do I start
Lazy lunch ladies
Can't be bothered to wash the dishes
By this time everyone had left
I couldn't stand it anymore
So I moved school
Unfortunately it happened again!

Olivia Haber (10)
King David Primary School, Manchester

6000 Years Ago

Sometimes I sit and wonder about things
I do not know what the earth was like
Know what the earth was like 6000 years ago!
Did spiders rule the earth?
Were deserts filled with snow?

I wonder what the earth was like 6000 years ago!
Did monkeys have a language which we just do not know?
I wonder what the earth was like 6000 years ago!
Was there some sort of creature who lived oh so low?
Or did us humans wear any sort of clothes?

I wonder what the earth was like 6000 years ago!
Did cats speak full English apart from the word no?
So really how are we to know what the earth was like 6000 years
ago?

Zander Davis (10)
King David Primary School, Manchester

My Worst Day Ever

In the morning I got out of bed
To go to the shed,
I then looked up and something fell on my head
I went inside . . . looked in the mirror . . .
I was not surprised . . . I had a bump on my head.

My mum put on some magical cream
Then she said 'Your head is filthy go wash it clean.'

So I went to the bath
And slipped on the mat
I fell head first
Then I was frightened of the big rat
So then I jumped up and bashed my head on the pipe
Which gave me a huge fright
Then I saw stars of light.

Sam Lawrence Gordon (11)
King David Primary School, Manchester

Late For Work

My children have done it again
What cheeky rascals they are
I tell them again and again
But they never seem to listen
Oh, when will my children learn
Never to mess with a clock.

I'm going to be stuck in traffic again
Come on get a move on
Everyone seems to shout
I'm stuck in rush hour again
I'm going to be late for work again.

My boss has called me in
What is going to happen?
Mr. Adams
You're late for work again.

Rafi Block (11)
King David Primary School, Manchester

Let's Go To Space

Let's go to space
And ride on the stars
Which planet should we go to?
How about Mars?

We will soar to Saturn
And slide around its rings
How about in a spaceship
We could sing!

We could go to the Moon
And hop like a bunny
We will be like spacemen
It would be so funny.

We will zoom like a shooting star
In the peaceful black sky
Climb into a rocket,
1, 2, 3 – we will be high in the sky.

We will meet all the aliens
Also the stars
We will sit by the Sun
It would be the best by far.

We could go to Pluto
And eat Milky Bars
We could go to Jupiter
And eat Mars bars.

This is a one time experience. Would you like to see?
This is an amazing world. Would you like to join me?

Eve Carruthers
Matthew Arnold Primary School, Liverpool

The Planets

The sun shines,
Onto the planets,
Mars, Earth, Jupiter and Saturn,
These are not original planets,
If you get too close,
You will experience madness.

The sun shines,
Onto the planets,
Mars, Earth, Jupiter and Saturn,
These are not original planets,
If you are happy,
You will experience sadness.

The sun shines,
Onto the planets,
Mars and more,
By the way,
These are not original planets,
Mars is boiling hot,
If you get too close you will get shot.

The sun shines,
Onto the planets,
Earth and more,
By the way,
These are not original planets,
Earth is cool,
So don't be a fool.

Ben Pauls
Matthew Arnold Primary School, Liverpool

Time

Isn't time peculiar?
For some it races by,
Isn't time strange?
How it really flies.

From the first minute of your life,
You want to grow up fast,
And when it's the last moment,
You wish you could go back to the past.

Seconds turn to minutes,
Minutes turn to hours,
The rain pours down,
As the seeds become gorgeous flowers.

That metallic golden sunrise,
You saw the other day,
Is a heavenly gift from God,
To wake you as you lay.

The joys in life are hidden,
You only have the key,
To unlock all of the lovely treasure,
For you and for me.

So enjoy life as it comes and goes
You only have one chance
As the sands of time ebb away,
Look forward, don't give your past a glance.

Amelle Turan
Matthew Arnold Primary School, Liverpool

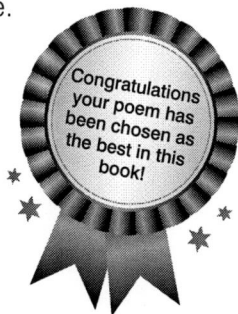

Congratulations your poem has been chosen as the best in this book!

Our Busy Day In Space

I went to Mars one day,
I met an alien called Ray.
We went to the stars,
And ate Mars bars.

Next was Saturn,
To slide on its rings.
Then we went to the Moon,
And we saw some incredible things.

We went to Pluto,
But oh no, we didn't fit.
So we went to the Sun,
For a bit.

We went to Jupiter,
It burnt our feet.
We went into a rocket,
And listened to a beat.

Down to Earth,
It was very cool.
Then I went to the amazing city of,
Liverpool!

We travelled to the Milky Way,
What a busy day.

Sadie Rietdyk
Matthew Arnold Primary School, Liverpool

Life's Law

Gaze into the air
Appreciate the sun flare
Little things you never saw
Come to life, life's law

See the Ferris wheel go round and round
The painted horses on the merry-go-round
See the ship just spin around
All those joyful children, shouting so loud

Look at all the cars, zooming so fast
All those rusty bikes – long they won't last
Those lorries over there, how proud they are
Buses dodging through traffic, taking us far

All those orange spring leaves, drifting by
The feathered birds, soaring sky high
Elated dogs, tails wagging
Tiny toddlers behind parents, slowly lagging

Once again, gaze into the air
Really look at that sun flare
Shield your eyes from that fiery glare . . .

Live your life without much care.

Jan Maciejewski (11)
Matthew Arnold Primary School, Liverpool

Imagination

We all have a power, a power that's inside
Some people like to show it
Others like to hide.

It's amazing, it's called imagination
Create . . . a lonely station?
Add a ghost – maybe two?
Wearing fancy high-heeled shoes.
How about a princess?
Dressed in pink, lilac and blue
With a smiley face so earnest and true.

Watch out!

Is she really what she seems to be?
No! She's a sea hag from the deepest, darkest sea!
There is no limit to our minds
We all have dreams of all different kinds.
You can create blue daisies, or glittery yellow heather
Compare anything with our minds and you'll find there's nothing better.

Quen Zhang (10)
Matthew Arnold Primary School, Liverpool

High In The Sky

High in the sky.
When nobody can hear you scream.
Let's go and hop on everything we see.
Let's go by every planet that we see and catch each star.
Every planet that we see will make a plan as will we.
We can make a pattern as we're by Saturn.
Live on Mars by the stars.
Let's go to Neptune as we listen to pop tunes.
Let's go to Mercury where it's hot and stuffy.
Let's go by Pluto and drink some luco.
Let's go by Jupiter and meet lumina.

Ryan Lalley (11)
Matthew Arnold Primary School, Liverpool

The End Of The World Won't End Us

You take me up into space,
I'm the luckiest person in the human race,
I feel like all the stars are mine,
I wait to be yours until the end of time.

I can feel the world spinning around,
It's as if you lift me off the ground,
I can see the stars in your eyes,
I can tell you there will be no lies.

We can dance on the Moon,
And let our hearts loom,
Next will be Mars,
There's no fault in our stars.

The Earth around us will disappear,
I'll survive as long as you're here,
Not even the stars can come between us,
Knowing you and I we'll never fuss.

Grace Jones
Matthew Arnold Primary School, Liverpool

Untitled

The wind howls around the creaky, old abandoned house.
That slumbers over the windy pathway.
The cellar is booby-trapped by sticky, gooey cobwebs that hang from
the ceiling above.
The ground floor is like it is guarded by the old, creaky wood,
That traps you down in the cellar like pets in a cage.
As this is the fright of Halloween night.
I hear a creak upstairs.
What do I do? What do I do?
Is it a zombie or is it a wolf?
What do I do?
I clamber up the stairs, as this is the fright of Halloween night.

Kian Fook-McGowan (10)
Matthew Arnold Primary School, Liverpool

Me In Space

I am in space,
It's like we're having a race.
I am next to the Sun,
I need to run.
Too far from Earth,
I am getting scared.
Heading for the Moon,
I am in a cocoon.
Let's go to Mars,
I can see the stars.
Let's go to Saturn,
I can speak Latin.
Let's go to Pluto,
I can play Ludo.
Let's go to Neptune,
I will listen to pop tunes.

Elenya Despoti (11)
Matthew Arnold Primary School, Liverpool

The World Around Us!

The Sun, the Moon, the stars, all up above.
Lying peacefully like a dove.
Reach the Moon, reach the stars.
You will see they're not like Mars.
Meet an alien, become best friends.
You never know where it ends.
Hop into a rocket with a friend.
Please don't make this end!
You maybe scared, you may be sad but just be glad.
You're in space, have a race!
Come on let's have fun! Don't just run!
Gravity's in the air everywhere.
Zooming, booming in the air above.
How amazing is the world around us!

Libby Grace Hazeldine (10)
Matthew Arnold Primary School, Liverpool

Space

We went to space one day,
We thought that we would stay.

We lived on Mars
Slept on stars.

We went to the Sun
Which was very fun.

We're going to the Moon
Very soon.

We're going to the Milky Way
Which is not that far away.

We'll go to Uranus
To make us famous.

Come with us I'm sure it will be fun.

Neve Sinnott (11)
Matthew Arnold Primary School, Liverpool

My Pet Star

My pet star is really nice,
But sometimes he can be as cold as ice,
He sits in my bed and lies on my lap,
But at night he does not nap,
He goes to space and plays with his friends,
He often tells me the fun never ends,
He slides on Saturn and bounces on Mars,
And when he does he flies past other stars,
He plays hide-and-seek and hides behind the moon,
And when he's on the dark side,
He discovered the dish and the spoon!
And when the morning slowly dawns,
My star comes back to me and yawns.
I love my star, I love him so, I never ever want him to go.

Ozan Turan (10)
Matthew Arnold Primary School, Liverpool

Moonlight And Saturn

M oonlight shines on the glittering stars
O h, let's go to the planet Mars
O h, maybe next we can go to Saturn
N ow we can make a cool pattern
L ovely stars on the planet of Pluto
I f you want energy get a bottle of luco
G reatness blooms on the Moon
H ey, let's go and make a boom
T he space is a wonderful place

S tars play on the Saturn ring
A nd it gives you that tingly thing
T he sky blooms as bright as stars
U nder and over the planet of Mars
R ound and round we go
N ow we can build a pile of snow.

Joseph Woodcock (11)
Matthew Arnold Primary School, Liverpool

The Fault Into The Night

The stars shine above the night,
The moon is beaming like the Sun reflecting on the clear water,
My head was looking up,
My eyes sparkled, all of the stars were perfect,
I smiled at them,
Then the Moon rose up,
I felt like I was in a dream,
I love every second that I took looking at them,
It felt like the stars lifted me up to space,
The galaxy was shining like little diamonds,
It really touched my heart when I watched every planet I glanced at.

Leshai Spooner-Gibbon
Matthew Arnold Primary School, Liverpool

Out Of This World

The air is thin and everything is so silent it's like nothing is going on.
But the planets are slowly spinning really slow, floating gracefully.
The stars are glistening and glowing but still silence responds to them.
You can float in space like it's invisible water surrounding you.
Saturn is a beautiful planet with its thin and rocky rings
And that's why it's the most beautiful planet and its gassy surface makes you sink.
Satellites float past taking lovely photos
That could give us important information about out of this world.

Daniel Bellham (11)
Matthew Arnold Primary School, Liverpool

Dream, Thoughts, Reality

Sunshine through the flames, the darkness shines brightly.
The Moon is far, Earth is near, I like to go there as long as I can see it.

I saw an alien fighting with the spacemen.

Three weirdos killed by the space alien, I celebrated with them -
They made me their captain of justice because we don't like bullies.

I can see the star far away from the bar, who knows what the future holds,
I have to wait until I become an astronaut.

Mansoor Ghaznavi (10)
Matthew Arnold Primary School, Liverpool

The Crazy Family Who Went Into Space

The crazy family who went into space,
Had a very big place!

They had a very hairy dog,
That likes to chew a log.

The dog was very smelly,
So he couldn't go into the rocket belly!

Then they set off,
Into the sky that's like a loft.

The car had steam coming out of it,
Like a smoking pit!

Finally they arrived,
Just like they have never been alive!

When they arrived they had a very big disaster
But one of the family members just wanted to watch Madagascar!

So they never got to see space,
Or their big place!

Emma Simpson (7)
Parish CE Primary School, St Helens

Untitled

Peace-bringer
Funny-singer
Black hole-creator
Crazy-driver
Air-taker
Moon-polisher
Planet-maker
Star-hanger
Planet-placer
Star-maker

Aliens!

Oliver Bond (9)
Parish CE Primary School, St Helens

The Weird Looking Alien From Outer Space!

There once was an alien,
Who always is called A Wailien.

He is always called A Wailien because he cries,
And he says that he likes the skies.

He was made purple,
Because he likes to gurgle.

He likes boxes because he is the shape of a box,
And his name is Lox.

He likes to eat curry,
Just like Andy Murray.

He likes saying hi,
Because he likes pie!

He likes dogs,
As well he likes logs.

Keira Martin (7)
Parish CE Primary School, St Helens

What Am I?

Morning-bringer
Joy-maker
Skin-tanner
Mind-blower
Flower-bloomer
Sweat-creator
Sand-softener
Sky-brightener
Cloud-chaser
Moon-remover
Craze-maker

The sun!

Jodie Louise Burrows (11)
Parish CE Primary School, St Helens

Planet Of Horror And The Alien Called Creepy

Creepy!

His name is Creepy,
And he is leapy, also weepy!

He lives in the 'Planet of Horror,'
That has a mighty warrior!

In the 'Planet of Horror' there is someone called Zog,
Also he likes to sit on a log!

He lives near the satellite,
That the aliens like to bite!

When they bite,
The bite has a lot of might!

The 'Planet of Horror' is green,
And they eat a lot of beans!

Ryan Foster (8)
Parish CE Primary School, St Helens

The Stars

The stars are blazing
I am gazing
Up in the sky
As the Moon passes by
Calms us down
Turns our frown upside down
Shooting stars make wishes come true
Leaves surprises for me and you
They give us light
Night by night
Daylight comes and the Sun is glowing bright
Don't worry they will back by night . . .

Kaley Harrison (10)
Parish CE Primary School, St Helens

Realm Of Cthulhu

The realm of Cthulhu is the lair of all the mobs.
Lurks the eye and brain of Cthulhu and the house of devilish gods.
With werewolves and zombies that lurk beneath your floors.
Watch out for the dragons that'll burn down your doors!
The goblin army and frost legion.
The pumpkin moon and skeleton!
The demonic bosses and relentless armies.
The realm of Cthulhu is all but friendly!
The eater of worlds, the destroyer,
The eye of Cthulhu and more!
Monsters live in caves and spawn at night.
They live there to give you a fright!
Dare you enter the darkest place in existence.
Then you are putting your life in danger!
Cthulhu's realm is the most dangerous place.
Monsters will jump in your face!

Callum Smith (10)
Parish CE Primary School, St Helens

An Alien Called Spook!

There was an alien called Spook,
And he read a book!

He took it to his crooked bed,
It was red!

He fell asleep,
And he had a weep!

He went to see his friend Zog,
And they sat on a log!

He went home in the dark,
And had a piece of bark!

He went home,
And got a phone!

Jamie Pimblett (8)
Parish CE Primary School, St Helens

Seasons

Seasons, seasons, we need seasons,
Without seasons the weather would be the same,
And that would be unimaginative,
So that is why we need seasons.

Winter, winter, is a chilly one,
Winter is a season where you need to wrap up warm,
Winter you need warm clothes on,
So get out your scarf and gloves and put them on.
Summer, summer, is a warm one,
Summer is when it's hot outside.
Spring, spring, is a cool one,
Spring is when flowers begin to grow.
Autumn, Autumn is a cold one,
Autumn is when leaves fall from trees.

Seasons, seasons, we need seasons.

Ebony Giles (10)
Parish CE Primary School, St Helens

Alien On Mars

There was an alien called Jack,
Who was black!

He lived on Jupiter,
He had a pizza.

He was miniature,
Also cute!

He watched stars,
On Mars!

He was square,
Also there was a mare!

They meet on holidays,
But not on Tuesdays!

Sam Nevitt (7)
Parish CE Primary School, St Helens

The Magical Space Land

The plum sky,
Which I saw with my own eyes.
A shooting star,
Races like a car.
A squeaking alien,
Having a funny conversation.
A huge planet,
With a big bonnet.
A colourful rocket,
Is as hefty as a giant's pocket.
The huge, buttercup Sun,
Whispered in my ear, 'I need to go now hun'.

Paige Nicholson (9)
Parish CE Primary School, St Helens

Aliens Into Space

Once there was an alien called Fred,
Who once slept on a wonky bed!

His skin was green,
It was the worst skin you have ever seen!

He liked to eat jelly,
And it gave him a big belly!

Fred likes to read a book,
But doesn't like to cook!

Fred likes to drink slime,
But doesn't like to drink lime!

Freya Lomas (8)
Parish CE Primary School, St Helens

The Alien

An alien with a hat,
With a pet bat.

Owned a house,
With a mouse.

The alien went to Mars,
And had some bars.

The alien likes Mars,
And he loved the cars.

The alien was called Trailen,
And he was a good alien.

Daryl Boyd (8)
Parish CE Primary School, St Helens

UFO

Do you know
A UFO?
Is it true
I don't know

Up high
In the sky
With the aliens
Flying by
Abducting people
Here and there
So you'd better *beware*!

Archie Chisnall (10)
Parish CE Primary School, St Helens

Untitled

I can see the sky
So fat with my own eyes
In outer space, I threw my lace
And people saw no trace
Then I threw my shoe
Into some goo
And it landed on the Moon
But it belonged to Neptune
'I hope I see it soon!'
So I'm going to zoom to the Moon
Like a rocket tomb.

Luis Newton (8)
Parish CE Primary School, St Helens

Beautiful Space

When you look at beautiful space, you have never seen such a place.
If you look at the stars, they will lead you to Mars.
The lonely, rusty Moon, is like a balloon.
The sun is bright, it gives you tonnes of light.
The Sun is flaming, who are you blaming.
Blast into space, because it's a beautiful place.
While the asteroids race, you go to your base.
The cats fly, while you dry.
The beautiful sky is dry.
The race begins in space.
Your base is safe, while you're in space.

Kyle Mather (9)
Parish CE Primary School, St Helens

Pailien The Dentist

I know a dentist called Pailien, that is an alien
And he loved to be called Tralian.

And he said . . .

Brush your teeth every day,
Then you won't get decay.

Brush them in the morning, brush them at night
Then they will be shining bright.

Follow these rules every day,
Then your smile will never go away!

Grace Murphy (8)
Parish CE Primary School, St Helens

Shining Star

Ssh, the Sun has gone the
Moon has come, it is time
For us to sparkle.
Time for us to start our
Daily job.
A way we go over the Moon,
Past the trees, over the horizon.
Right it is now time to go, I
Can not wait for a new
Morning to dawn.

Chloe Taylor (10)
Parish CE Primary School, St Helens

Outer Space

The rough, bumpy Moon looks like a white balloon.
In space there are lots and lots of glowing stars.
If you went to space you could see Mars.
In space the aliens there are thin and green, spooky creatures,
Blue, friendly and even happy aliens with one eye.
There are lots of planets like the Moon
That is like a spoon.
In space there are tonnes of nights – they are very magical.
In the dark space you can't play the chase.
Space is a race.

Ben Wilkinson (8)
Parish CE Primary School, St Helens

Sweetie Planet

When you go to space,
And you stand on the Moon,
Next to the star above you,
You will see a planet called Sweetie Planet.

You get lots of weather,
The rain is lemonade,
The sun is an orange bonbon,
The snow is mints,
And the clouds are candyfloss.

Ella Fox (10)
Parish CE Primary School, St Helens

The Big Huge Moon

The big, huge Moon
Who had a spoon!

The Moon is grey,
Because it likes to pray!

The Moon is great,
Because it likes to wait!

The Moon is tearful,
Because it is cheerful!

Eleanor Ward (7)
Parish CE Primary School, St Helens

The Blueberry Moon

The blueberry moon is bouncy like a bed,
It has seven candyfloss suns
Which are fluffy like a puppy.
Its chocolate coat is runny like water,
Inside the moon it's squishy and squashy
Like a mashed up strawberry.
The suns are small like mice,
The look of the chocolate coat is brown like mud
And everything is perfect.

Jessica Baxter (9)
Parish CE Primary School, St Helens

Who Am I?

Morning-breaker
Sweat-comes
Flower-bloomer
Hosepipe-bringer
Light-creator
Sports-appearer
Mind-blower
Tan-maker
Beach-buzzer.

Kyle Hamon (10)
Parish CE Primary School, St Helens

An Alien

Mum! Mum! There's an alien upstairs!
Charlie! Behave there's no such thing!
Mum! Mum! Come quick, it's big and hairy,
Like what your legs look like before you shave!
Charlie! Behave yourself!
Mum! Mum! It's going over to . . .
Charlie stop telling porkie pies!
Mum! Mum! Oh it's ok.
It's just my little sister looking at me!

Caitlin Wild (10)
Parish CE Primary School, St Helens

What Am I?

Twilight-sparkler
Night-watcher
Star-gazer
Daylight-slither
Light-changer
Sleep-maker
Sun-remover
Mind-blower.
The moon.

Sophie Jasmin Vickery (Arnold) (11)
Parish CE Primary School, St Helens

Untitled

5, 4, 3, 2, 1, blast into space, because it is a wonderful place!
You will have such fun, and you will be sad when it is done.
There is a planet called Mars and around there's lots of stars. (but no cars!)
You should see the Moon, and quite soon.
(And when you're on it), play an instrument on the Moon
And it will make a lovely tune.
Stand on the Moon and you will be as light as a balloon floating in space.

Alexandra Mercer (8)
Parish CE Primary School, St Helens

Super Food Planet

In a deep gloomy universe a million miles away.
Is a bright joyful planet called Super Food 10157195.
The population is 1,557,101,197.
People are gummy bears.
Mud is icky, sticky, gloopy chocolate,
Clouds are fluffy marshmallows,
Rain and the sea are lemonade, snow is white tasty icing sugar,
Mountains are liquorice and crocodiles are spiky tacos as spicy as ghost chillies!

James Peel (10)
Parish CE Primary School, St Helens

Moon

The pale Moon's bright light is like white snow
Resting in the distance.
The Moon lights up the dark sky at night
Observing the world and everything around it
Every night the Moon is bright
But never helps you to see in the night light.
The children observe the Moon
Every night they watch the Moon.
Every night they imagine the Moon with a face.

Ben Unsworth (11)
Parish CE Primary School, St Helens

Untitled

The lonely Moon looks like a white balloon if you look up.
If you look up at the stars they lead you to Mars.
If you look up to the Sun you're about to burn!
When you look at beautiful space you have not seen such a place.
The sun is bright, It gives you a burst of light.
The Sun is flaming, who are you blaming?
Blast into space because it's a beautiful place.
Whilst the asteroids race you go to space, your base.
The craters fly while you dry.

Jamie-Leigh Unsworth (8)
Parish CE Primary School, St Helens

Who Am I?

At night they lurk around in the cornfield
They like bees and leave signs in the field.
They come from the planet Mars, they have a ship
Their ship is a funny shape, a funny shape indeed.
They can blend in with everyday objects.
Their breed is unknown – a mammal, an arachnid? We don't know.
How did they get here, we didn't see them coming
They must have a cloaking device.
They are a generation ahead in technology.

Connor Etchells (10)
Parish CE Primary School, St Helens

Outer Space Land

When I look into the ebony sky,
I can see all the stars,
In the sky up high,
I can also see the crimson Mars,

A glowing, shooting star,
I saw an emerald spaceship,
Races like a zooming car,
The spaceship is as tiny as a lip.

Holly Palmer (9)
Parish CE Primary School, St Helens

Untitled

Star-hanger
Darkness-bringer
Moon-polisher
Air-taker
Alien-maker
Black hole-creator
Astronaut-floater

Space!

Amy Burke (9)
Parish CE Primary School, St Helens

What Am I?

Puddle-maker
Risk-taker
Crash-creator
Flood-spreader
Hazard-Inventor
Storm-producer
Umbrella-igniter.

Sam Briscoe (11)
Parish CE Primary School, St Helens

Elemental Island

In a galaxy far, far away
There is a planet called Elemental Island.
The planet is split into 4 quarters, the people can control rock
Their homes are made of rock too.
In the fire quarter the people can control lava and fire.
They love to be near cacti
That's why their homes are made of it.
The people in the fire element are completely made out of lava!

Luke Cain (10)
Parish CE Primary School, St Helens

Mars Bars

One day Mars,
Went out to get some bars
Once there was an alien named Zog,
He likes to eat frogs.
There was a Mars bar in the bin,
I wanted to eat it but I put it in the tin.
Mars fills jars,
Full with bars.

McKenzie Sturgess (7)
Parish CE Primary School, St Helens

Chewy Gooey Planet

Chewy Gooey planet
Chewy Gooey planet is full of cheeky gummy bears
But also gummy floors, walls, doors and windows
And if you land on this vermilion, colossal planet,
All gummy bears will come and say hello.
This planet is as gummy as 5 million chewing gums.
With its population 21,210,
Chewy Gooey Planet is the planet where you will love to be.

Kieran Langlois (10)
Parish CE Primary School, St Helens

My Dream Of Space...

The dark sky is beautiful
Down my eye came a tear
An alien came and told me
'Space is amazing . . . I know dear.'
The plum sky lay down
The stars shone up with love
I disagree how you could frown
All this lovely sight up above.

Kayleigh Houghton (9)
Parish CE Primary School, St Helens

Shooting Stars

Shooting stars are truly amazing,
You can see them when you go star gazing.
Like a comet up in the sky,
Floating around way up high.
We stare at you star,
Who comes from afar.
You look just like a laser beam,
Shining bright like a twinkling dream.

Caitlan Holden (11)
Parish CE Primary School, St Helens

What Am I?

Shining bright
Raging crimson,
Scorching, blazing,
reflection-creator
Way above
Gleaming stars
Blinding everyone
All day long.

Abbie Brown (10)
Parish CE Primary School, St Helens

Untitled

Blast off to space and you will see it's a lovely place.
Some people say the Moon is made of cheese.
The Moon is quite dusty so it will make you sneeze!
Float off the Moon and you will meet your doom!
Float in space and there will be a massive Earth chase.
Play an instrument on the Moon and it will make a lovely tune.
Stand on the Moon and you will be as light as a balloon.
Float in to space.

Olivia Mahon (8)
Parish CE Primary School, St Helens

What Am I?

Night-brightener
Sun-remover
Sleep-maker
Eye-shutter
Curtain-closer
Body-rester

The moon!

Lewis Martin (10)
Parish CE Primary School, St Helens

Untitled

The lonely Moon looks like a white balloon.
Space has a beautiful face.
On the Moon I'd like to be soon.
All of a sudden I saw an alien!
It was ugly, slimy and mostly gross,
And it was getting really close.
It ran into the ship and the ship was a tip.

Femi Heald (9)
Parish CE Primary School, St Helens

The Night Sky

An amazing amethyst sky
It is so beautiful I cannot lie
I see stars glistening in the night
When I look up I see the stars that sparkle bright.

I saw a shooting star
It went so fast it looked like a racing car.

Ella Elizabeth Roberts (8)
Parish CE Primary School, St Helens

Moon

Pale shimmer all through the night.
No one around just the Moon shining bright.
Far away beneath the clouds so white an illuminating presence of light.
Shooting stars flying by the Moon as children making wishes so soon.

George Graham (10)
Parish CE Primary School, St Helens

Untitled

Space has an ugly face.
The elegant stars, light up Mars.
All of a sudden I saw an alien,
It was colourful, clever and green.
The sky is always high.
In space there is gravity so you can fly.

Angel Louise Chapman (9)
Parish CE Primary School, St Helens

What Am I?

Shining bright
Quickly Moving
Radiating light
Flying high
Making sight
Eye-catching.

Holly Rhoden (10)
Parish CE Primary School, St Helens

Out Of This World!

Stars are shining ever so bright,
Shining stars through the night.
Shooting stars, make a wish,
Give you life – a little twist.
Flying across the azure sky,
A trail of stardust left behind.

Ross Davies (10)
Parish CE Primary School, St Helens

Lovely Stars

S hining brightly all day long
T winkle, twinkle amazing star
A lovely view you are
R ising in the sky
S ee you soon stars.

Asha Susan Chowdhury (7)
Parish CE Primary School, St Helens

Acrostic Poem

S hooting stars in the night
P lanets ready to be explored
A liens in their spaceships fly
C limbing the Moon and space discovery
E verybody wants to catch a glimpse.

Megan Brown (11)
Parish CE Primary School, St Helens

Space

S hooting stars like fireworks on bonfire night.
P lanets orbit like a bike wheel in the Tour de France.
A liens zooming like people in rush hour.
C reatures creep slowly into their habitat.
E veryone's gazing like there's a diamond in the sky.

Adam John Lewis Ball (11)
Parish CE Primary School, St Helens

The Planet Of Excitement

Space is big, space is wide, it makes everyone petrified
The floor in space is icky and sticky
It makes everyone feel very sicky.
In space it's a really good place.

Rhys Howells (10)
Parish CE Primary School, St Helens

Shooting Star

Shooting star in the sky,
How I wonder how you fly?
Do you swash?
Do you swish?
Can you fly to the moon?
While dancing like a loon?
Can you fly from moon to Mars?
Or fly past all the stars?
Can I see you in the sky?
Or can I see you shooting by?
Shooting star in the sky,
How I wonder how you fly.

Jasmyn Sahota (10)
Prenton Preparatory School, Prenton

My Friend Stars

I once went in a rocket
Flew right up to space
I saw an alien
Who walked in an alien pace

He waved at me
So I flew down
He greeted me
He was colourful and brown

I said to him
'Aren't aliens green?'
He said 'Not al all,
That is only the Queen'

The things he showed me
Like food and drinks
I met one of his friends
Who was slimy and called Winks

We jumped up high
And landed on Mars
I then asked him his name
He said it was Stars

I said 'Where's your mother?'
He said 'Over there'
I looked over there
She was munching on a pear

I said 'Where's your father?'
He said Over here'
I looked over here
He was drinking some beer

We then reluctantly said goodbye
And I sadly flew off into the sky.

Amelia Booth (10)
Prenton Preparatory School, Prenton

I Would Love To Go To Space

I would love to go to space,
I would take a big, red suitcase.
Once I got there,
I would eat my juicy, green pear,
Then fly to sunny Mars,
And see the bright sparkly stars.

Then I would go for a long walk,
And meet a purple, spotty alien who talked.
We would go to the bubbly Moon,
Hopefully it wouldn't go *boom*!
After that we would travel around the Milky Way,
And go to the alien bay.
I gave him a ball of Playdoh,
He gave me a big, sparkly bow.
He landed on a star,
And bought a great big Mars bar,
We gobbled it all up,
Then we played with his rubber duck.
Then we went to the ice cream shop,
And had some bubbly pop.

We went to see his school,
And saw his best friend, called Tool.
We went to the space pool,
It was so, so cool.
We each did a fancy cartwheel,
Then we had a massive meal.

I said goodbye
And whizzed off in my rocket, into the sky.

Mirren Wood (10)
Prenton Preparatory School, Prenton

Match On Mars

On the planet Mars
There was a set of bars
A stadium lies
With a lot of cries
It was Galaxynian FC
One of the players saw me
His name was Polycocian
Team Jupiter was there
His face was a pear!

The day had come again
The referee, Chen
And finally the whistle blew
The ball went that way, the ball went this way
The crowd know it will be a long day
The managers went crazy
A few of the players were lazy
The striker moved forward, no doubt he would score
The goalkeeper saved the shot and the crowd went bore.

Goal, goal, goal!
Unfortunately it was time to go
But I said no.

Keyanmehr Norouzi (10)
Prenton Preparatory School, Prenton

The Girl In Space

There once was a girl who went to space,
And that was pretty ace!
She went around calling and falling and then crawling,
And that was pretty ace!
She started to say 'Hey, hey, hey!' but no one was around,
But there was only one sound and that was a hound.

Hannah Pettener (10)
Prenton Preparatory School, Prenton

The Clumsy Moon

There was a clumsy moon,
He was a total baboon,
He would clash into Jupiter and Mars,
They called him a dars,
He was just a little moon.

'Hey, come over here,'
'No, my dear,'
'I'm not your dear baboon,'
At that moment the moon fell in doom,
'Just come over here!'

The moon in a hurry came to the Sun,
He had a job which he wanted done,
The moon cried in a hurry,
His best friend, Pluto, gave him a curry,
Then he made fun.

'Off to the mission' said the void,
'Yeah' said the moon, who said 'void,'
'Argh, will there be food?' said the moon,
He was in total doom,
And that's the end of the moon.

Andrew Wicher (11)
Prenton Preparatory School, Prenton

The Small Green Alien

I once went to space, it was a gigantic place.
I met a small, green alien from planet Scalion.
The alien was small but very wise and tall.
He took me to the base it kind of looked like a face.
He showed me how to surf then I flew back to Earth!

Olivia Lynch (10)
Prenton Preparatory School, Prenton

Little Alien

In a galaxy far away,
An alien used to spend his day,
Chillin' and chillaxing by the sun.

Then one morning while he was zooming and zagging,
He crash-landed on Earth and saw lots of people surf.
The alien saw a big, big house,
Suddenly a mouse scurried out.

Then out stepped a girl about the age of ten and a little boy called
Ben.
They said to the alien 'where did you come from?'
And then he replied 'Space.'
They started to walk at a normal pace and stopped,
The girl gave the alien a locket and he stepped into his rocket and
zoomed away,
Far, far away.

Keira Adams (11)
Prenton Preparatory School, Prenton

Space Giants

Oh black hole, black hole, what did you eat?
Black hole, black hole, it must have been meat?
Was it car or was it plane?
Black hole, black hole, or was it a train?

O galaxy, o galaxy, what do you hold?
Galaxy, galaxy, it must be a planet or was it a star?
O galaxy, o galaxy, you drive a black car,
O galaxy, o galaxy, you are very far, o galaxy, o galaxy
I'm looking at you through a bar.

O planet, o planet, what do you see?
O planet, you look like a pea
Planet, o planet, I look through a scope
And take you a bar of thick, silky, smooth soap.

Alex Hall (10)
Prenton Preparatory School, Prenton

Tummy Of Joy!

In the tummy of joy,
I found a digested doughnut,
Covered in chubby chocolate.
I saw silky skin,
With wrinkly wrinkles like a granny.

I heard the tummy rumbling rough,
Like a loud lion scaring things off.
I lost my green glove,
In the lanky pipe of mystery.

I smelled a prickly pasty,
Lurking at the bottom of a deep fall.
I felt a smooth, brown bun,
Hiding away from danger.

I tasted a crispy crisp,
Lovely with taste.
I spied a duffy doughnut,
Zooming around.

Atshaam Ashraf
St Anne's RC Primary School, Manchester

The Raindrops Alien

R epulsive rain, it smells like mud.
A s stinky as a dinosaur.
I t eats a man, as greedy as a pig.
N o one talks to him because he is naughty.
D rops his drink, which
R ains like a meteor.
O bviously has a party every day, and
P arties like a DJ. Then goes to bed and
S inks like a rock.

Nana Kojo Adjei Kusi
St Anne's RC Primary School, Manchester

Animals – Insects

A ntelopes eating ropes
B unnies are quite funny
C amels made the towels
D ogs made the lucky logs
E lephants met the cuddly infants
F rogs – the relatives of long logs
G rasshoppers won't do a stopper
H amsters on the big bannisters
I nsects on a horrifying shipwreck
J ellyfish are quite stiff
K angaroos met a cool dude
L lamas ain't no calmers
M onkeys eat anything nice and chunky
N ewborn kitties are so pretty
O tters go mad for dots
P arrots like polka dots
Q ueen bees are so busy
R ats being chased by cats
S nakes living in lakes
T om cats getting the sack
U nicorns they saw
V iper – always a biter
W ater hogs, little clogs
X -ray chickens won't stop lickin'
Y aks – scared of bats
Z ebras with levers.

Celiece Campbell (9)
St Anne's RC Primary School, Manchester

The Close Finish

Entries were over as the cars get ready for the starting area.
Wheels are going like a charm,
Engines are ready to take down the roads.
Each car was ready to race.
The race lights turned red.
The count down has begun.
Lights are turning yellow.
20 cars, three winners, let's see who will win...
The lights were green and they're off!

They are all racing for the gold trophy or a chance to get on the podium.
Cars are going around the first curve and there have already been three wipe outs!
Crowds were shocked at the crash while the remaining cars pass the first lap.
This isn't an original type of situation, this is the world cup!
Cars are going with the wind but one went too fast and made a wipe out!

There goes the 3rd lap and things are going pretty smooth.
Five cars are hitting each other and make a total wipe out!

4th lap takes its place and the cars have a destruction going on.
Making the final lap will determine the potential finalists.
It's the final stretch!
Wow, what a close finish!

David Kayembe-Kaniki (10)
St Anne's RC Primary School, Manchester

Monkeys

I walk in the jungle and this is what I see
A troop of monkeys staring at me

Banana skins everywhere
With no pears
'Where is Mummy monkey? Oh look she's over there!'

Daddy monkey, Dave
Lives in a tree.
He was desperate
So he went for a pee.

Baby monkey, cheeky Charlie
Plays all day
But Daddy monkey, Dave
Makes sure he doesn't run away

Mummy monkey stays at home
And cleans the xylophone
The day at the jungle was long
And smelt of monkey pong
It was good
Even though I kept on standing in mud.

Ellie Louise Gavin (10)
St Anne's RC Primary School, Manchester

Space In Action

Flawless stars twinkled brightly
Galaxies twirled in a ballerina's show
Aliens hopped across a planet
Black holes smacked her lips hungrily
Meteors crashed into each other
They bump, crash and roll
Astronauts petrified of aliens
Walking like zombies

Stars brightening up the sky
The planets rotating round
And round
Slow or fast
Rockets zooming all around
Making you dizzy.

Maria Ozuzu
St Anne's RC Primary School, Manchester

The Cave Of Nightmares

In the gloomy cave of nightmares
I saw a haunted, cursed person
As I walked up to him
He had red eyes with blood on his mouth
I was as scared as a wimp
So I ran further into the cave

I approached a random and spooky-looking door
But I opened it without hesitation
As I entered there was the beast
And he was having a little feast

Then he saw me and thought I was a feast
So I ran away from the beast
As I got out of the cave I saw my friend, Dean.

Daniel James Davis (10)
St Anne's RC Primary School, Manchester

Ronaldo's House

In Ronaldo's house of happiness, I found Ronaldo's clean kit in his bag.
I saw all of his cool achievements in his cabinet.
I heard his son called Ronaldo Jr playing on the Xbox online.
I lost his football CR7 boots and found them.
I smelled his wife cooking special food.
I felt his proper clean kit, it was so amazing.
I tasted the food, it was so awesome.
I spied a trophy falling around the place.

David Igbinosa
St Anne's RC Primary School, Manchester

In Greggs Of Joy

I found a pasty
I saw it, it looked nasty
I heard it was supposed to be lovely.
I lost the very nasty pasty
I smelt a sausage roll, it was nice
I felt it, it felt like rice.
I tasted it, the cheese and onion pasty,
I spied on it later, lastly.

Liam Moloney
St Anne's RC Primary School, Manchester

Space

S pectacular space
P erfect aliens
A ttractive moons as they sparkle
C areless martians shouting 'Arhhh'
E xcited stars as the moon flies past.

Holly Lawrence (9)
St Anne's RC Primary School, Manchester

Untitled

Sun, oh sun, how do you do?
You're a very swarming sun!
Are you a sad sun?
But I think you are a spectacular sun
And a sanguine sun and a very still sun.

Eryn Hodson
St Anne's RC Primary School, Manchester

Space

S parkling stars, oh, they're so bright
P luto does not produce much light
A stronauts go there all the time
C ool as the chocolate bar the Milky Way is
E xciting place space can be.

Molly Keyes (9)
St Anne's RC Primary School, Manchester

The Life In Space

Our green friends awake on planet Mars, sweating like an oven,
Looking down to Earth, searching for food.
With four eyes, hot cooking human,
Keeping strange things,
They are very different to us,
They hide in massive holes, hiding from extinction,
And hiding from the hot helium coming from the core of Mars,
Waiting for sight of a human,
Looking for supplies,
Trying to catch a rocket.
Some day our green friends will come down to Earth,
And fit in well with us,
Helping us and being our friends.

Joshua Evans (10)
St John's CE Junior School, Manchester

The Man And The Alien

There once was a man,
Who liked to eat ham
And dream about going to space,
He dreamt of the Moon,
And going there soon,
But not before cleaning his face.
He saved up to buy a rocket,
With money from his pocket.
He went straight to Mars,
And came back by the stars,
And decided to stop on the Moon,
He floated around not hearing a sound,
But suddenly out of the blue there came into view,
A strange rocket all shiny and new.
Out popped a creature all slimy and green,
Who jumped back inside so he couldn't be seen,
'Hello' said the man,
'Would you like some ham?
We can eat it while we look at the stars.'
The creature came out with a cooked trout,
And they both started to eat tea,
'It's lovely and quiet' said the creature to the man
I came by the stars
And passed you on Mars.
What a lovely journey I've had.

Emma Lily Connolly (10)
St John's CE Junior School, Manchester

Unlucky Wally

Once upon a time, long ago,
There lived a man you might know.
This man was extremely unlucky,
And everywhere he went he got rather mucky.

Oh poor Wally, you are so unlucky.

He gets bugs up his ear,
The man next to him smelt of beer.
Wally loved a girl across the road,
But he thought she wouldn't love someone who looked like a toad.

Oh poor Wally, you are so unlucky.

But the girl had a boyfriend, she waved to him and said goodbye,
Poor Wally started to cry.
One day Wally had a nap,
A bunch of maggots went in his cap.

Oh poor Wally, you are so unlucky.

Wally met a girl and said 'Marry me,
We will live together happily'.
They were both as ugly as each other,
But still they loved each other.

Oh happy Wally, you are now happy!

Millie Connolly (10)
St John's CE Junior School, Manchester

Milky Way

Hey, hey, you ever heard of the Milky Way?
You're a loon if you've not heard of the Moon.
Earth is a planet but can it be as hot as the Sun?
Don't touch it that wouldn't be fun.
Saturn's ring now that's real bling.
I'm Isabelle Place and I know a lot about space.

Isabelle Place (10)
St John's CE Junior School, Manchester

My Space Buddy

Every Saturday morning I make my way to space,
Accompanied by my best friend who's got a purple face.
His hands are webbed, he's short and fat,
He always wears a cowboy hat.

He comes from a planet called Kazob,
I can't say his name so I call him Bob.
When I first met him it was rather dark,
He crashed his ship into the park.
We fixed it together, we made it right,
He asked did I want to go on an adventure tonight?

He took me to space, he showed me the sights,
The creatures on Uranus gave me such a fright.
We had so much fun, we became such good friends,
We promised that this would not be the end.

So every weekend off we would go,
Where we would end up we didn't know.
We visited Jupiter, Saturn and the stars,
And on the way we had milkshakes on Mars.
Of all the places that I have been shown, like Dorothy said,
'There's no place like home!'

Hannah Hobin (9)
St John's CE Junior School, Manchester

Yummy Space

Space so far, far away
Full of twinkly stars and unicorns
Full of yummy Milky Ways and Galaxy bars
Full of Mars bars and lollipops
And a very big, hot gobstopper
I love the popping candy as it
Whizzes through space
The lion has a lovely time
Leaping its way through yummy space.

Isabel Massey (10)
St John's CE Junior School, Manchester

Cosmic Creation

Shooting stars, whooshing comets and marvellous meteorites.
Pitch-black skies that come alive at night.
Like a twinkly blanket as I close my eyes.
I fall asleep dreaming of space delights.

Little green martians and the Man in the Moon.
Oh how I would love to meet them,
I hope it's someday soon.
I could speak to them in martian and I could walk on Mars,
Exploring the whole galaxy with no holds barred.

When I grow up I'll be an astronaut,
and launch a rocket into space.
I'll travel through new galaxies and cross the Milky Way,
and fly home on Halley's Comet and be there and back in just one
day.

Oh to be a spaceman,
If all my dreams come true.
Floating around in zero gravity,
and flying a rocket too!

Owen Gill (9)
St John's CE Junior School, Manchester

Out Of This World

Out of this world there are people who walk on their heads.
Out of this world there are snails that eat beds.
Out of this world rabbits swallow chewing gum.
Out of this world elephants make mud pie.
Out of this world pandas tell lies.
Out of this world children tell adults what to do.
Out of this world adults wear one shoe.
But my world is the best!

Teja Kiala (10)
St John's CE Junior School, Manchester

Our Solar System

Starting with Mercury the smallest of all,
This planet's so hot it will frazzle them all.
Then there is Venus the brightest you'll see,
Named after the goddess of love and beauty.
Next is our Earth of which we call home,
And we're thankful for what is has done.
Mars the red planet with deserts all round,
Similar to Earth of which we have found.
Then we have Jupiter filled with gas,
Which at any minute could have a blast.
Up next is Saturn also filled with gas,
With a rocky dust ring, to see it is a must.
Now it's Uranus, no not your backside,
This is a planet that has a dark side.
Here goes for Neptune, named after Roman god of sea life,
It is the ice giant for all to see.
And last we have Pluto, surrounded by five moons,
furthest from the sun.
I hope you had fun because now I am done.

Mason Hughes (10)
St John's CE Junior School, Manchester

Family

Family is forever
No matter how low the valley
Or how impossibly high the mountain may appear,
Your family is forever,
Death is as inevitable as birth
And our family will grow
In Heaven and upon the Earth,
Our loss is an angel's first flight.

Tiffany Hayley Allen (10)
St John's CE Junior School, Manchester

Space

Space
Such a big, dark, silent place
With objects floating here and there
There is no gravity or no air.

Astronauts wear special suits
With big helmets and heavy boots
Rockets blast them into space
Setting off from a special base.

Nine planets orbit the Sun
Earth is the humans' only one
The Sun is our very great big star
Seen in the sky but very far

Special robots sent to Mars
To look for life signs just like ours
What's out in space I do not know
But I'd really love to go.

Alex Ambrose (9)
St John's CE Junior School, Manchester

Little Alien

I am a little alien,
I come from outer space,
With long thin legs and gangly arms,
And a small, round, funny face.

I am a little alien,
I come from outer space,
I crashed my spaceship on the Earth,
When flying in a race.

I am a little alien,
I come from outer space,
I need some help to get me home,
To Mummy and my base.

Tom Burton (9)
St John's CE Junior School, Manchester

Rainbows

A multicoloured arch that forms in the sky
A spectrum of colours, red, orange, yellow, blue let's not forget
indigo and
violet too.

Rainbows, rainbows in the sky glistening in the cloudy, misty sky.

Not an object, never physically touched, made by angels to put your
mind at
rest and peace on earth.

Rainbows, rainbows in the sky glistening in the cloudy, misty sky.

Like magic you appear reflecting and bending in water droplets in the
atmosphere so high, just as you magically appear throughout the
day, no time
for wishing, no time for wandering, how near, how far, like a blink of
an eye my
rainbow disappears.

Amani Shad (9)
St John's CE Junior School, Manchester

Earth Invasion

They came to Earth at night,
Hiding behind bushes and trees.
With only their antennas in sight,
And laser guns hanging from their knees.

They started roaming in the day,
They were looking for one special man,
They wanted to take Simon Cowell away,
And have X Factor on planet Spam.

They found Simon Cowell in his mansion,
And took him back to planet Spam.
They planed another Earth invasion,
Simon told them 'Get the Louis Walsh man'.

Cameron Mollitor (10)
St John's CE Junior School, Manchester

To Be An Astronaut

Oh, to be an astronaut, to fly so high in my rocket
Exploring the planets, asteroids and moons,
While looking out of the window where earth looms,
With the eight planets in the solar system in sight.
I would be sailing to them like a bird in the night.
Mercury, Venus, Earth and Mars,
Are our terrestrial planets amongst the stars.
While Jupiter, Saturn, Neptune and Uranus,
Are the gas and ice giants on the outer sides.
Each has it's own features; individual and great.
With mountains and moons, rings and lakes.
To fly around them and sail by,
In this wonderful adventure above the sky.
There is nothing more fantastic for me.
Oh, to be an astronaut!
Wow, things I would see.

Antonio Turner (10)
St John's CE Junior School, Manchester

Above The World

A bove the world which is dark,
B ut the sun lights it up,
O ver the Sun is the solar system
V ibrant planets you see,
E ven the planets have a living!

T rue there's nine,
H eaven is close by,
E ven planets have a family,

W hat a world to explore!
O ver the Sun is the solar system,
R ockets, stars and more
L ook over there! I saw a twinkle,
D on't go to bed too early! You might see above the world!

Grace Todd (10)
St Luke's CE Primary School, Oldham

Solar System And Space

S aturn with rings
O ur solar system is amazing
L ight is shining
A steroids launching up, up and away
R ockets launching up, up and away

S pace is interesting
Y ou and me spinning
S tars are sparkling
T itan is a moon
E ndless spinning
M ars is so hot and red

and

S hooting stars in the sky
P luto standing all alone
A stronauts landing on the Moon
C omets hiding and shining
E ndless spinning is so hard.

Laaibah Imran (10)
St Luke's CE Primary School, Oldham

The Sun

A morning-waker
A cold-taker
A warm-helper
A burning-ball
A glowing-stall
A big-boss
A freezing-loss
A golden-commander
Big fun . . . I am the sun.

Emily Kerwin-Royle (9)
St Luke's CE Primary School, Oldham

85

Space Is Alive

Mercury is an angry man
Mars is a mountain giant
Earth is a memory winner
Jupiter is a friend of Saturn
Saturn is getting married
Uranus is boss of Neptune
Neptune picks on Pluto
Pluto is always lonely.

Lilia Mercado (10)
St Luke's CE Primary School, Oldham

Space

S olar system
P lanets listen
A steroids
C oming this way to
E arth.

Amber Faulkner (9)
St Luke's CE Primary School, Oldham

Space!

S un owns us
P luto is an old friend
A red-eyed man runs at us
C an you see us out tonight
E ven though we're not that bright?

Demi Darlington (10)
St Luke's CE Primary School, Oldham

Mission To Mars

A mission to Mars
From the human planet Earth,
Zooming up so high.

Lilia Smith (9)
St Luke's CE Primary School, Oldham

Into Space

Up into the sky
I do feel like I can fly
Is that Mars? Oh my . . .

Charlie White (9)
St Luke's CE Primary School, Oldham

Our Planet

Our planet is loved
Even aliens could come
We would care for them.

Luis Mercado (10)
St Luke's CE Primary School, Oldham

Space

In the solar space
The planets roam the darkness
Whilst rockets zoom past.

Maria Ahmed (9)
St Luke's CE Primary School, Oldham

The Romans

Celt-killer
Gold-greeter
Jewellery-maker
Road-builder
Sword-stabber
Fearsome-fighters
Spear-throwers
Bridge-builders
Armour-wearer
Royal Roman
Crop-stealer
Gory-gladiator.

Grace Kettle (9)
St Margaret's Anfield CE Primary School, Liverpool

The Romans

Inspired inventors
Tactical slayers
Jewellery-makers
World-conquerors
Sword-slashers
Shield-heavers
Heavy drinkers
Grape lovers
Gods-worshippers
Slave-collectors
Gold-seekers

Kostas Kuklys (9)
St Margaret's Anfield CE Primary School, Liverpool

Untitled

Celt-crusher
Roman-worshipper
Iceni-hater
Celt-killer
Army-fighter
Roman-ruler
Gold armour
Steel armour
Sword-swinger
World conquerer
Rotten Romans.

Bradley Wasley (8)
St Margaret's Anfield CE Primary School, Liverpool

Boudicca

Roman-hater
Roman-wrecker
Red-haired killer
Slave-taker
Money-maker
Crazy-fighter
Man-hanger
City-ruler
Gold-wearer
Head-tearer
Sword swinger.

Ella Dooley
St Margaret's Anfield CE Primary School, Liverpool

Boudicca

Trouble-maker
Roman-slayer
Head-ripper
Eye-poker
City-ruler
Roman-hater
Arrow-deflector
City-protector
Money-maker
Fierce looker.

Francis McCabe-Madden (9)
St Margaret's Anfield CE Primary School, Liverpool

The Romans

Empire-guarders
Golden armour
Sword-swiper
Celt-killer
Battle master
Country-conquerers
Clever thinkers
City-rulers
Strong warrior
Wine winners.

Libby Barr (9)
St Margaret's Anfield CE Primary School, Liverpool

Boudicca

Sword-slayer
Dagger-holder
Crazy killer
Roman-wrecker
Gold-wearer
Eyeball-popper
Poison-drinker
Bad thinker
Roman-hater
Roman-slayer.

Jocelyn Culshaw (8)
St Margaret's Anfield CE Primary School, Liverpool

The Celts And The Romans

A golden warrior
Weird looker
A sword-slasher
A shield-heaver
A poison-drinker
Mosaic-makers
Bridge-builders
City-rulers
Money-makers
Danger-followers.

Ben Blackham (8)
St Margaret's Anfield CE Primary School, Liverpool

Boudicca

Bloody killer
Sword-stabber
Poison-drinker
Gold-wearer
Fearless fighter
Spear-thrower
Roman-killer
Colchester-conquerer
Money-maker
Roman-wrecker.

Emily Richardson (9)
St Margaret's Anfield CE Primary School, Liverpool

Boudicca

Roman-defeater
Pride-protector
Tribe-ruler
Fierce-looker
City-burner
Head-turner
Clever thinker
Poison-drinker
Village-carer
Enemy-destroyer.

Ella Jones (9)
St Margaret's Anfield CE Primary School, Liverpool

Boudicca

Roman-wrecker
Poison-drinker
Spear-thrower
Head-chopper
Blood-painter
Shield-shover
Land-lover
Ground-breaker
Brain-shaker
Slave-waker.

Aaron Hampson (8)
St Margaret's Anfield CE Primary School, Liverpool

Boudicca

City-protector
Roman-slayer
Celt-ruler
Child-killer
Fire-thrower
City-burner
Roman-hater
People-helper
Clever thinker
Revenge-taker.

Kaylyn Grace Dawe (8)
St Margaret's Anfield CE Primary School, Liverpool

The Celts

Poison-drinker
Bad-thinkers
Sword-stabber
Roman-wrecker
Mad-painter
Roman-hater
Insane-inventors
Roman-bruiser
Celt-ruler
Bad-footer.

Laurie Stowers (8)
St Margaret's Anfield CE Primary School, Liverpool

Boudicca

People-protector
Enemy-detector
Injury-maker
Roman-hater
Clever thinker
Poison-drinker
Celt-ruler
Country-ruiner
Revenge-taker
Trouble-maker.

Abbi-Lynn McGovern (9)
St Margaret's Anfield CE Primary School, Liverpool

A Roman Soldier

Distance-runner
Flame-thrower
Celt-killer
Object-maker
Boudicca-hater
Man-killer
City-invader
Trouble-maker
Manly fighter
City-builder.

Ruby Belle Davies (8)
St Margaret's Anfield CE Primary School, Liverpool

Boudicca

Child-killer
Roman-hater
Celt-ruler
Fierce-looker
People-protector
Pride-owner
Money-stealer
Ground-shaker
Poison-drinker
Weak fighter.

Leah Power (9)
St Margaret's Anfield CE Primary School, Liverpool

A Roman Soldier

Manly-fighter
Flame-maker
War-owner
Country-invader
Distance-runner
Trouble-causer
City-builder
Order-shouter
Peace-bringer
Flame-thrower.

John-James Evans (9)
St Margaret's Anfield CE Primary School, Liverpool

Boudicca

People-protector
Child-killer
Celt-ruler
Roman-hater
Revenge-taker
Fierce looker
Celt-fighter
Head-turner
Sword-fighter
Neck-strangler.

Tassyana Silveria-RSmith (8)
St Margaret's Anfield CE Primary School, Liverpool

The Romans

City-winner
Sneaky fighter
Sword-stabber
Roman-ruler
Crazy Celts
Great gladiators
Great inventors
War-winners
Great skills
Horrid killer.

Holly Mason (9)
St Margaret's Anfield CE Primary School, Liverpool

The Rotten Romans

Sword-slashers
Marching marauders
Inspired inventors
Spoilt slayers
Evil emperors
Rotten rulers
Diving daggers
Country-conquerors
Iceni-haters.

Jack Anthony Robinson (9)
St Margaret's Anfield CE Primary School, Liverpool

A Roman Soldier

Man-slayer
Order-shouter
Iceni-hater
City-maker
City-protector
Arrow-deflector
Enemy-destroyer
Empire-bringer.

Daniel Porter (8)
St Margaret's Anfield CE Primary School, Liverpool

Boudicca

Celt-ruler
Roman-taker
Fierce looker
Roman-hater
People-protector
Poison-drinker
Child-killer
City-burner.

Brogan Courtney Towner (9)
St Margaret's Anfield CE Primary School, Liverpool

The Celts

Sneaky Celts
Crazy killer
Poison-drinker
Golden-wearer
Roman-stabber
Red-haired killer
Neck-ripper
Red and green-wearer.

Gabrielle Thomas (8)
St Margaret's Anfield CE Primary School, Liverpool

Boudicca

Roman-hater
Child-killer
People-protector
Roman-killer
Celt-ruler
Fierce looker.

Rida Fatima (8)
St Margaret's Anfield CE Primary School, Liverpool

Celts

Naked fighter
Barbaric slayer
Horrible eater
Man-hunter
Throat-ripper
Sacrifice-taker.

Daniel McDermott (9)
St Margaret's Anfield CE Primary School, Liverpool

Boudicca

Roman-hater
Sword-stabber
Drinks-poisoner
Queen-killer
Crazy killers
Dagger-holders.

Sydnie Foster (8)
St Margaret's Anfield CE Primary School, Liverpool

A Roman Soldier

Country-invader
Boudicca-hater
People-slaughterer
Trouble-causer
Empire-bringer
Distance-runner.

Frea Rose Beth Johnston (8)
St Margaret's Anfield CE Primary School, Liverpool

Boudicca

Roman-hater
Clever thinker
Celt-ruler
Poison-drinker
Money-maker
City-destroyer.

Katie Millington (9)
St Margaret's Anfield CE Primary School, Liverpool

Stars

Loudly, now the blue silver stars;
Were loitering on the special black bars,
They called it the universe of colours;
Not just because it was like no other,
But the silvery bright, dusty round moon;
Was now crying into her silvery shoon,
This golden planet with a fiery heart;
Pierced by the red-hot sun like a dart,
The colours all show their small faces;
Without any coloured, shadowy traitors
Space was engulfed in golden stars;
They were driving around in silver cars.

Jorja Grace Lily Miller (10)
St Mary's CE Primary School, Manchester

Space

Thousand miles from the ground,
Jupiter, Venus, Mercury and Mars,
Spiral round as fast as a spinning top,
Silent, snoozing space sleeps,
The sphere planets are a basketball,
Moving – moving -
Are they emotionless?

Space is a shadowed cave,
Sparkling, shining, glistening stars,
Blinking, glimmering on Earth,
Stars are like shiny, smiley faces,
Glimmering in the night sky,
Are you a lonely moon?

The moon is alone,
Circling around the Earth alone,
Alone?
He thought never!
A commodious grey balloon,
Spinning – spinning,
A commodious grey balloon,
Is like a scenery spiralling,
Is the moon alone with the stars?

Mercury, Venus, Jupiter and Mars
Are all the planets below the stars,
Mars is a boiling, scorching surface,
Venus is a grey, misty haze ball,
Jupiter is a colossal hole,
Mercury is a hole in the wall,
Is this real space?

Caitlin Jones (9)
St Mary's CE Primary School, Manchester

Magnificent Moon

Are you lonely moon?
You giant, white balloon,
You have no water, wind or air,
You're alone like a cloud with no rain,
Do you want to be my friend?
I do . . .

Slowly you light up the night sky like a lightbulb,
Lonely lights you make, which illuminate down to Earth,
Please moon don't cry,
You rule all kinds of stars like no one.

Quickly and quietly, you send me to your star,
It is lovely to see you smile,
You have not smiled in quite a while.

Lift me to your idol,
Venus, Mars, Jupiter and especially the Milky Way,
Is that your dream, to be him?
Red, yellow, shiny blue perfect orange as sweet as the sun.
It spins like a colourful spinning top -
Spinning – spinning.

Suddenly it approaches,
The thing that kills all kind,
'Quick run!'
Turning, turning,
'Gulp that was nice.'
The black hole spoke.

The black hole is a tornado,
A black and dangerous tornado,
Above the clouds,
And away from Earth,
The tornado twists,
Twists and twists.

The stars hide,
And illuminate the dark sky,
They are shiny, smiley faces,
Blinking at you through your transparent window.

Silence remains while space goes to sleep,
Again and again it carries on,
Goodnight!

Faith Megan Robinson (10)
St Mary's CE Primary School, Manchester

Moon

Are you lonely moon?
You giant white balloon
You look so pale,
Please don't wait and please don't wail
I will find you a friend.

I went to fly
When something caught my eye
Zooming to the black heavens spaceships were off
'Was it true?'
'Was I there?' I asked,
While the stars were dancing.

Shall I go or not?
Shall stars be his friends?
Nah! I thought, *no way!*
Let's do another adventure.

Suddenly, I saw the blue star
It was not far
Shall that be his friend?
'Yes!' I cried, 'That will do!'
Come on star there's the moon.
Please come he needs you
You're coming with me.

Rachel Phillips (9)
St Mary's CE Primary School, Manchester

Space

Silent, sleeping space,
The land of dreams,
Are you lonely sun?
You from the Earth you're no longer than a bun.

When I look up into the stars,
Mercury, Venus and Mars,
They all are basketballs moving,
Moving, moving, moving.

Space is a pitch-black canvas waiting to be painted,
Everyone waited,
Down on Earth,
Like a bullet shot the comet . . .

Red dragon,
That's the best one,
Makes the sky have a picture again,
As it goes in one lane.

Also another best one,
But it's come and gone,
The fantastic luna eclipse,
Makes everyone have a lisp.

Mars is a scorching hot surface,
Venus is a massive grey rock,
Jupiter is a massive planet,
This is space . . .
Goodnight space.

Kiera Massey (9)
St Mary's CE Primary School, Manchester

Space

Space is an enchanted land of dreams,
Waiting to be discovered.
It is filled with wonderful nature,
And your dreams fill you with happiness,
It is unimaginable.
Sleeping, silent space is as beautiful as the singing heavens.
The colossal rocket zooms up to snoozing space with a roar.
Cavernous Mars,
Are you best friends with the twinkling stars?
Scorching, golden sun,
You're like a great big yellow bun.
Great white moon, you're so much better,
Than my little sister who's such a bed wetter.
Venus is a tough red dragon
Even bigger than my dad's ancient wagon.
The brown chocolate bars,
Stand tall and tower in great Mars
Smiling, the blinding-gold sun,
Waves at the cold moon
Space is real!

William Guy Nixon (10)
St Mary's CE Primary School, Manchester

Stars

It was on a starry night, shining bright,
Twinkling stars flashing at midnight;
This way and that they run across the sky,
Now dusk comes and dawn says goodbye;
Shooting, flashing, twinkling all night,
Now the moon comes and the stars shine with light,
The bright stars were like diamonds in the sky,
As the shooting stars pass by while they fly;
The outer world is a marvellous place,
Mars, Jupiter, Saturn and more – they are the planets of space.

Mille Hooper (11)
St Mary's CE Primary School, Manchester

Space

Space is an enormous black canvas waiting to be painted,
Space is a land of the unknown waiting to be discovered,
The stars dance around the illuminated night sky,
The moon's face sparkles in space,
The sun beams out rays of light to make the world shine.

Are you lonely moon?
You great, white balloon,
You have no wind, water or air,
How can you live without any hair?

Stars do you live with enormous red Mars,
Do you live by eating scrumptious yummy chocolate bars?
Do you live in a dark gloomy haze?
Do you count for endless days?

Sun you are a golden bun,
You weigh quite a tonne
You keep us all alive
You look like a beehive.

Matthew James Rupert Dickinson (10)
St Mary's CE Primary School, Manchester

Sparkle

Shining, bright stars sparkle the way;
Walking the night into the day;
Stars create a river of light
Which fills the darkness of the night

One by one the twinkling stars
Guide the way to the Planet Mars;
Sparkling stars dash across the sky
The Milky Way says its goodbyes

As flying stars pass on today
They shall be back, trust me I say.

Lucy Barrett (10)
St Mary's CE Primary School, Manchester

Stars

Slowly, silently now it's dark;
The luminous mystery
Returns with her glistening sparks
Large silhouettes hover around;
The tall, black sea without a sound
The winking stars in the night sky;
Glaring down like they're never shy.
As the sun returns stretching high;
The stars leave and say their goodbye.

Phoebe Tootell (11)
St Mary's CE Primary School, Manchester

Nebula

Slowly, silently, now it's night
Here's a small clouded mystery
It's in my line of golden sight
As you cautiously roam alone
Space is your brand new empty home
I wonder about your past history
As the sun returns flying high
At day all your stars say goodbye.

Casey Myers (10)
St Mary's CE Primary School, Manchester

Shine Above Me!

A giant spray of orange paint in the vast topaz sky.
Like an enormous ripe orange hovering in the sky like it's ready to be picked.
It is a roaring fire shining on a freezing cold winter's day.
Giving you the warmest of hugs as you leave the beautiful beach
Glittering, illuminating, shimmering.

Daisy Grace Goddard (9)
St Mary's CE Primary School, Manchester

Shimmering Stars Shining

Glistening, illuminating, the stars are a glittering blanket surrounding the galaxy.
Like a sparkling engagement ring twinkling in the golden sun.
Shooting stars are high-speed marathon runners flying across the inky-black night sky.
Gleaming stars give a reassuring wink promising your wildest dreams will come true.
Dazzling stars shine on me and you.

Phoebe Caine (9)
St Mary's CE Primary School, Manchester

Beyond The Moon

Slowly, the galaxy reveals his glow
Looking like a clown's dickie-bow
Silently twinkling, the stars float
Like the sun glistening on a moat
Pink, blue and black, the sky emerges from his natural shades
Carefully, gradually, it all fades.

William Henry Marshall (11)
St Mary's CE Primary School, Manchester

Rocky Terrors

Large lumps of rock quickly hurtling round the immense galaxy
As bitter as a perishing iceberg sinking the Titanic
A rushing torpedo soaring around the Milky Way
Wrestling through the inky sky with deadly foes!
Perishing, gargantuan, impressive.

Thomas Matthew Jarman (9)
St Mary's CE Primary School, Manchester

Driving In The Past

I'm driving in the past
I'm going really fast
I think I have a rash
I hope I don't scratch
Or else I'm going to cry
I'm in the future
I'm taking a picture
I hope I don't fail
Or else I'll climb up the rail
I'm in the train
I'll go down the drain
I hope I don't shrink
Or else I will stink
I'm a mole
I'm in the North Pole
I finally found some coal
I'm really happy
I'm that flappy
I am frozen
So are a dozen
I'm in the night
Mum says sleep tight
I know how to tweet
I love sweets
I'm in the car
I've got a scar
I hope I don't cry
Or I give a big sigh.

Samuel Adeoye (9)
St Patrick's RC Primary School, Manchester

Year 4 Classroom

Mr Dooris is the best
Better than the rest
Other teachers don't do magic
That's why Year 4 are fantastic.

The pupils are great
And we are all good mates.

Holy statue
I think I'm gonna aaa achoo,
'Oh my, bless you.'

Such a polite girl
Best in the world
Such a pleasant boy
Year 4 filled with joy.

Zoe Price
St Patrick's RC Primary School, Manchester

Spring

Leaves are growing everywhere,
Flowers blossom over there.

When you see the flowers here,
You will go complaining to people near.

One beautiful morn,
The flowers are born.

The lambs are running,
The bees are buzzing.

Another day,
I'm shouting hooray.

Sky is blue,
Cows shouting moo!

Niat Kahsay (8)
St Patrick's RC Primary School, Manchester

The Magic Potion

One day a boy called Jon,
Made a magic potion.
He put in so many things,
Human eyes and bat wings,
He even put in his mum's rings,
His brother's shoe
And a bottle too,
Even a tiny mouse,
Until it went *boom!*
It blew up the house.
Hair, wings, eyeballs everywhere
All the potion went in the air.
His attempt at magic
Was very tragic.

Sonny Drake (9)
St Patrick's RC Primary School, Manchester

Who's The Best?

I am the best,
Better than the rest,
I live in a house,
And people think I'm a mouse,
Because I am small,
And they are tall,
I drank a potion,
And had a notion,
That I was a mouse like,
Too small to ride my bike,
I am too small to tie my lace,
While I'm in a mouse race.

Darren Njomo (9)
St Patrick's RC Primary School, Manchester

Winter

W inter is a fun season because you can go
  I n the snow and it is
N ice and it only lasts for
T hree months like every other season
E ven though winter is the
R ight season for fun.

Yaruuna Lkhagvajav (8)
St Patrick's RC Primary School, Manchester

The Life Of A Star

In the beginning, it felt like the end.
An atom formed, called hydrogen.

Hydrogen gave us the light, stars and
The big fireball that helps us live.

The sun it is, the holder of seven planets.
Sooner or later it will go mad.

When a star runs out of its fuel,
It loses balance and goes cool.

An explosion happens called supernova,
It releases energy and makes a black hole.

This black hole sucks everything in,
The energy of it means that light can't escape from it.

The time slowly passes and the big point loses its mass.

It's slowly getting smaller until it collapses.

And some of its hydrogen gas escapes,
And the cycle repeats all over again.

Kacper Hagedorn (10)
Sedgley Park Community Primary School, Manchester

The Fascinating View

Majestic meteors as fast as a fly go into the sky
As my space craft as large as a plane flies.

Fascinating colours of the star crust sparks up space
But unfortunately has no face.

The moon smaller than the sun is grey and old
It's been stepped on many times and has a circular mould.

Earth had a life and is larger than the moon and surely does have faces
While it spins round in the fascinating view of space which in it has some spaces.

Galaxies with many solar systems are all over the place
While there's discoveries in space.

Comet shower raining down on the ground
Coming out of its bound.

Aliens . . . why
Why are you so high?

Samir Hussain
Sedgley Park Community Primary School, Manchester

Solar System

S tunning blasts of scattered bright colours
O n-board a floating steel rocket
L ight beaming, peaceful around the Earth
A liens . . . No, just solid rocks and airless dust
R ocks burning to death by the beaming sunlight

S hooting stars bring light to the peaceful Earth
Y oung aliens walking around the huge planets
S olar system looking focused on the Earth
T eleporter whizzing into future and past
E xtraordinary stars crashing into the galaxy
M oon been shaped on by heavy weighted people.

Hasan Gohar (11)
Sedgley Park Community Primary School, Manchester

Planet Space

As I fly through the sky
I gaze as I am ever so high
As I walk on the majestic moon
I see sparkling stars ever so soon
The elegant Earth below me is so small
It looks just like a bouncy ball!

Jupiter's moon looks as wavy as the sea
Someone's quite amused and that's me
Blue, purple, pink too!
Everyone needs this, they really do!
Come and explore this wonderful world
See the planets that will have been swirled!

Come and see the colourful crater
Whoever designed it is a wonderful painter!
As I return down to Earth
This was the most marvellous moment since birth!

Haneeah Warda Fazel (10)
Sedgley Park Community Primary School, Manchester

What Am I?

Life-giver
Boiling gas
Shining sun
Round ball
Breath-respirator
Water-boiling
Spot, round
Ice-melter
Snow-burner
Bees-giver
Volcano-warmer
Day-bringer

The sun.

George Eze (11)
Sedgley Park Community Primary School, Manchester

What Am I?

Chill-bringer
Cold stinger
Meteor-watcher
Flag-holder
Darkness-destroyer
Silver-shiner
Chubby ball
Tide-controller
Swift spinner
Ship-hater
Nebula-liker
Eternal-liver
Earth-befriender
Space-watcher
Sun-liker

I am the moon.

Adeel Malik (10)
Sedgley Park Community Primary School, Manchester

My Space Adventure

As I fly through the sky
I notice that I'm ever so high!
As I land I can see
All the spectacular stars above me.

As I step forward onto the moon
I am amazed of what I can do so soon.
Down below me the Earth is so small
It feels like I'm the biggest of all.

The dazzling nebula that's the best
It's much more colourful than the rest.
Blues, pinks and purples too
Everyone needs to see them, they really do!

Zainab Patel (10)
Sedgley Park Community Primary School, Manchester

Magnificent Moon

What am I?

Darkness-taker
Light-bringer
Flag-blower
Night-approacher
Helpless-grower
Life-giver
Silver-shiner
Cold-stinger
Air-collector
Human-holder

The moon.

Emaan Mohammad (10)
Sedgley Park Community Primary School, Manchester

A Journey Into A Black Hole

The gases are swirling around a black point
From rocky horizon, to the night sky
I see a large . . . massive, in fact, sphere rising
The swirl disrupts the Earth's atmosphere
And is gradually turning into a planet, devastating moment of judgement . . .

I'm getting closer and it's getting hotter
I'm coming through the event horizon
There's nothing but pitch darkness . . .

Weronika Okwieka (10)
Sedgley Park Community Primary School, Manchester

My Space Quest

S hooting stars crashing into the darkness that covers the night sky!
P eaceful galaxies floating endlessly to their mysterious worlds.
A stronauts coming in their space shuttles, bombarding different galaxies.
C old skies lurking over, watching contentedly.
E vil aliens once roamed and didn't rest, they came to conquer but now they are gone . . .

Danyal Uddin (10)
Sedgley Park Community Primary School, Manchester

Amazing Space

S hooting asteroids burned by the sun
P icking space rocks from the space
A liens . . . no, just you're shadow
C rashing asteroids making me feel as scared as a mouse running away from a cat
E scaping from the world of asteroids, my 'mission to go home.'

Antoni Magon (10)
Sedgley Park Community Primary School, Manchester

The Cow That Stepped On The Moon

The cow took a deep breath,
He took a step on the moon
And he was the first cow to step on the moooon,
He left a footprint,
And he was the first cow to leave a footprint on the moooon,
He saw an asteroid,
And was the first cow to see an asteroid on the moooon,
He mooed so loud,
And was the first cow to moo on the moooon,
He went home in a rocket and he was the first cow to survive on the moooon,

Zaid Al Sayed (9)
Temple Primary School, Manchester

My School Day In Space

I got up, brushed my hair
It was 8am, then I met my friend,
At 8.50am we went to the sun and saw an alien having fun
By 10.50am we were on Mercury, with an alien who said he can cure
you and me!
11.10am, the end of break and we were close to Venus,
But then I met an alien who was very mean to us.
Back on Earth for lunch.
There wasn't just one alien but a whole bunch!
At 1.30pm, after launch (ha, ha)
We arrived on Mars, where that mean alien was being put behind
bars!
Then on to Jupiter, the aliens were even more stupider
Next on Saturn, we collected the baton, for the Olympic Games
Touch down on Uranus,
Where the aliens were ready to avenge us
Through the gloom shone Neptune
Our final stop we saw a forbidden planet called Pluto.
But that only left me 20 minutes to get back to school!
At 3.20pm I arrived back to school,
To hear my friends tell me to stop playing the fool!

Fazil Khan (10)
Temple Primary School, Manchester

Planets

The planets go around the sun,
One by one they go,
It starts with Mercury, Venus, Earth and Mars,
These are the planets near the stars,
There is also Jupiter, Saturn, Uranus and Neptune too,
Then there is Pluto but we can't see you!
There are eight planets that we know,
One by one they go . . .

Imaan Hussain (10)
Temple Primary School, Manchester

The Planets Of The Solar System

There are eight planets that orbit the sun,
Mercury is by far the smallest and closest one,
Next comes Venus, shining bright,
It's the second brightest one,
Then Earth, the most important one,
The planet where you and I come from!
Fourth is Mars, an icy, red planet,
That's surrounded by stars,
Following on, Jupiter which is the biggest planet,
That spins the fastest with an amazing 63 moons!
The grooviest planet is Saturn with rings of rocks, dust and other things,
Uranus should be filled with pride, a unique one, that lies on its side,
Last but not least, Neptune,
That usually has stormy nights,
These are the planets of the solar system,
Different climates for each one,
But one thing in common,
They all orbit the sun!

Nadia Khairuddin (11)
Temple Primary School, Manchester

Mission X – Train To Be An Astronaut

Saturn, Jupiter and Mars, Mission X, reach for the stars!
Mission X revolves in space, trying to find an alien race!
Girls, boys and teachers too, Mission X, is for me and you!
Anti gravity and having fun, Mission X reach for the sun!
Little Pluto the smallest one, even smaller than the sun!
Comet, galaxies and the Milky Way, everyone having a fun day!
Stars, stars up so far, nobody knows where you are!
Temple Allstars having fun, whilst doing their missions under the sun!

Hafsah Iqbal (10)
Temple Primary School, Manchester

My Very Energetic Mother Just Served Us Nine Pickles

Mercury, the first of them all,
Then it's Venus, the slightly bigger ball
Earth is third, with mixed weather
On comes Mars, hot enough to burn a feather
Jupiter, it can't be fitted into a box
Saturn follows on, surrounded by rocks
Uranus is next, big and cold
Neptune comes after, it could make you bald!
Pluto the not so big ball
It is bisected from the rest, and surrounded by a wall
These are the planets, some are generous, some do really bite
But there's one thing they all have in common
They could easily give you a fright!

Mahmood Sewehli (11)
Temple Primary School, Manchester

Mission X

Mission X it is so cool,
If you don't like it you must be a fool!
Space it is so cool,
You've got to go to space ace . . . ace . . .
Constant constant little light,
How I wonder why you are so bright
But now I know you are a satellite!
That sparkles through the night, ight, ight!

Ali Choudhary (9)
Temple Primary School, Manchester

Stand In Space

Here I am stood in space
Thinking, *where am I?*
Asking myself, 'Where is the best place?'

Is it the sun?
Maybe not
It's so hot
I might look like a melted pot.

How about Jupiter?
Yet it's so big
Not much to eat
Not even a fig.

Let's go to Saturn
It's still so great
I'll invite my friends
And we'll have a play date.

I like the sound of Neptune
But it's so cold
I have a feeling when I leave
I might be bold.

Here I am on Uranus
I managed to keep my hair
I'm very hungry right now
I could do with a pear.

I don't like these planets
Apart from Mars
But I might go back to Earth
Just for a Mars bar.

Here I am back in space
And I think I found the right place.

I'm at the best place I can find
It's a bright star
But there is one bad thing
I lost my car.

Mia Goodwin (10)
The Heys Primary School, Ashton-Under-Lyne

From Mars

Space is the place,
To learn and see,
Filled with
Amazing geography.

The stars, the comets, the meteors
Wait a second – there is some more,
The Earth, the moon and the sun,
Isn't this so fabulous and fun?

The stars twinkle and
Illuminate in the sky,
The comets constantly,
Whizz and fly.

A meteor is bits of rock,
If you learn about space,
This wouldn't
Be a shock.

The Earth has jungles,
Rocks and lakes,
The moon is so exciting,
You tremble and shake.

The sun is so vivid,
It will hurt your eyes,
So don't be dumb,
Look away – be wise.

Having read my poem,
You have learned about the stars,
So if you like to meet me,
I'll be waiting on Mars.

Maya Mistry
The Heys Primary School, Ashton-Under-Lyne

I Forgot My Space Gear

I was in the rocket
Ready to blast off to space.
But my dad said,
'You forgot the cup cake,'
Which was mashed up in a bag.

And then a few minutes later,
My mum said,
'You forgot your helmet
From under your bed.'

But then my sister said,
'Your oxygen
Is on the kitchen windowsill.'

After that
My brother said,
'You forgot the energy from
The garden.'

And then my leader said,
'You're fired.' But I found
My cup cake that my dad said
Was mushed up in a bag.
And it was delicious.

Kian Adam Schofield (10)
The Heys Primary School, Ashton-Under-Lyne

Space Is The Place

Space is the place that is ace,
Stars set above your love.

Look at the planets ahead,
Some gas, some rock and maybe ice.

Don't fall in the deep black hole,
If you do you could lose your soul.

Mohammad Qais
The Heys Primary School, Ashton-Under-Lyne

I See Space!

5. Radio
4. Check
3. Buttons on
2. Uh-oh! I'm moving
1. Blast off!

I'm in trouble, I thought, as I thought I heard a crash,
I panicked then I went to investigate,
And I found myself on the rocky moon.
I see the sun,
A roaring ball,
In the space wall,
It's that hot if you land,
You will be dead in seconds.

Jupiter, Mercury, Venus and Mars,
I like eating Mars bars,
Planets so hot, like Venus or the sun,
You can't resist the fun.

Did you know Uranus has diamonds,
Aliens love diamond as much as they love you.

Saffie Sadiq
The Heys Primary School, Ashton-Under-Lyne

The King Of The Skies

Shooting stars shooting by like a firefly.
They burn through the atmosphere, they see the moon.
'The eagle has landed.'

They jump out, Neil Armstrong, the first man to land on the moon.
They clutched the flag and jammed it into the moon's surface.
Apollo 11 has been completed
It took three days to get there,
With only 40 seconds of fuel left to get there.
Their footprints will remain now in the cold, dark dust.

Hannah Lily Davies (9)
The Heys Primary School, Ashton-Under-Lyne

All About That Space

I look up at the sky and see,
All the planets staring down at me.

The stars twinkle and the sun shines,
I can see shooting stars at times.

There is a big place, which is outer space.
You need a big pocket, to get there by a rocket.

You will see a star, but you will have to be afar.

You will then see the moon,
Also known as the lune.

I travelled there by a rocket, but I forgot my house locket.
I went to the sun, just to have a bit of fun.

Saturn has rings, it's used for its bling.

Jupiter has a lot of gas,
But that's not all, also a lot of mass.

Another place to discover out of this world.

Kartik Joshi
The Heys Primary School, Ashton-Under-Lyne

My Journey Into Space

Because I'm flying past Mars
I can see the spectacular stars
Whizzing past black holes acting gloomy and mysterious
I wouldn't go in it.

Going back to Earth
No aliens I have seen
Landing on sweet Earth
Finding sweet green.

Jake Andrew Walker (9)
The Heys Primary School, Ashton-Under-Lyne

Exploring Space...

There is the rocket,
Blazing through the air,
Going to the moon,
Has lots of craters.

Captain, something's not good,
The oxygen tank is empty,
And there we go,
Round and round.

In space,
We arrive on a planet,
Which was red and had ice,
And has rocky boulders.

We float in the air,
And there we go,
We have a problem,
Are you even listening to me?

Shazeb Akbar
The Heys Primary School, Ashton-Under-Lyne

My Space Journey

I'm going into space,
It's supposed to be a great place.
Can't wait to find out
What a black hole is all about.

Gonna see the stars,
While I'm flying past Mars.
Space is mysterious,
The sun is serious.

The sky is pitch-black,
I'm staying on NASA's track.
Astounding sights, my jaw drops,
Oh no! Out of fuel . . . my rocket drops.

Tia Mistry (10)
The Heys Primary School, Ashton-Under-Lyne

Dreaming Of A Space Trip

Yuri Gagarin orbited the Earth
Sat on a cushion because he was as small as a Smurf
Neil Armstrong, he was a loon
Deciding to to be the first man on the moon.

Back at the Soviet Union
Yuri enjoyed a great reunion
Apollo 11, the moon mission
Neil ready at the intermission.

View another race!
Last man in space
Could this be you
Joined by your courageous crew?

I'm now in space
Waiting to see an alien's face
Suddenly I hear something at the spaceship's door
It was my mum and I was so full of bore!

Mohammed Awais Hassan
The Heys Primary School, Ashton-Under-Lyne

Untitled

A roasting hot boiling ball
Turning red quickly
Flames fly out like lava
In the dark mysterious space
It is roasting red and orange
Like in a frying pan.

Bailey Thomas Greenwood (10)
The Heys Primary School, Ashton-Under-Lyne

The End Of The Universe!

Black holes hauling gravity from the ground,
People panicking, bolting around.
Earth getting sucked closer, what should we do?
People don't know – is there a clue?

Risk-taking scientists trying to find out,
What would happen if the black hole moved about?
Screaming and crying, babies wail,
Could the black hole ever fail?

Breaking up Earth, breaking up space,
Could Earth ever be a habitable place?
People dying, such a tragic day,
Could this happen again like today?

Black holes blanking, wearing down,
No one, not even a mouse, is in town.
All muted, all silent, all clear,
Is there even anything left to hear?

Aimee Burrows
The Heys Primary School, Ashton-Under-Lyne

Apollo 11

Jupiter explodes,
A black hole forms,
Mars starts spinning,
Out of control.

People panicking,
Running away,
Nearly planets,
Whizzing past,
The black sped closely.

Snout beats quickening,
On the edge of space,
Jupiter stretching,
Into a black hole,
Like a giant tornado,
Pressure smashing,
Then sudden silence.

Logan Troy Riley Robins (10)
The Heys Primary School, Ashton-Under-Lyne

Me And The Planets

Space is the place for me and you,
Come with me and you will see the stars above,
And if you look so far away,
You can see the biggest planet in the solar system.

If you would come with me,
From the beginning you would see,
Mercury,
Venus,
Earth,
Mars,
Jupiter,
Saturn,
Uranus,
And Neptune!
And sing a song to make a tune,
You will never forget.

Millie Roberts
The Heys Primary School, Ashton-Under-Lyne

The Planets

A burning, flaming hot sphere,
It flashes like lights in a room,
It's in the centre of our solar system,
We love to see it in summer time.
It's our glorious, heated sun!

It spins on it's side,
It is identical to our Planet Neptune,
People say it's a gas giant.
It 's our frosty Uranus!

It has a rocky core,
It has eight phases.
It's our gloomy, gloomy moon!

It is identical to our Planet Jupiter,
Its rings are 169,800 miles wide.
It's the Planet Saturn!

Adeena Rehman (10)
The Heys Primary School, Ashton-Under-Lyne

Don't Stay On Jupiter!

Don't stay on Jupiter, it's airless
Don't stay on Jupiter, there is no food
Don't stay on Jupiter, it's made out of gas.

Don't stay on Jupiter, it has way too much gravity
Don't stay on Jupiter, it has a great dark that is called 'the eye' of Jupiter
Because it's very stormy there.

Don't stay on Jupiter, it's poisonous and deadly
Don't stay on Jupiter, it's too hot
Don't stay on Jupiter because if you try to walk on the ground
You will sink and get destroyed.

Don't stay on Jupiter, it's too big
Don't stay on Jupiter the atmosphere is too thick
Don't stay on Jupiter, it has large oceans in which you cannot swim.

Qasim Malik (10)
The Heys Primary School, Ashton-Under-Lyne

Above The Atmosphere

There is a glowing
Red, extremely hot
Sphere-like flame
In deep space
Gazing at the sun.

In the NASA station
There is a
Celebration for
The people who
Went to the moon.

We went to Mars to
Eat a Mars
For it was
Full of dusty sand.

Tej Lad
The Heys Primary School, Ashton-Under-Lyne

Out Of This World

When I am older I want to go into space,
Cause I might bump into a monster with a very funny face.

It might be an alien
It might be big and scary,
What if he had lots of eyes,
And his chin was very hairy?

Maybe they could swim,
Or some of them might fly,
Or some might even walk up in the sky.

Some might have spots,
Some might have stripes,
Some might be harmless,
Some might like fights.

I imagine lots of monsters and aliens to see,
But my imagination must be wrong.
Cause when I got there
There was no one there but me.

Charlotte Williams (8)
West Kirby Primary School, Wirral

The Solar System

S tars are asteroids on fire
O rbits surround the planet
L anding rockets from all around
A stronauts flying away
R ockets zoom into outer space

S pace is dark and cold
Y ou can zoom to the moon
S atellites were made by men
T ravel to outer space
E arth is so amazing
M ars is red like lava.

Max Browne-Daley (8)
Westvale Primary School, Liverpool

My Trip To The Moon

Look at the moon, it looks like cheese,
Can I go Mum? Oh please, oh please,
I'm only nine, I have my suit,
It's an all in one with silver boots.

Mum said no,
But I still want to go,
So I made a rocket out of tin,
Now my journey will begin.

Off I went at the speed of light,
My face looked baggy, what a sight!
I landed on the moon, it was jerky,
Oh, I wish I had gone to Mercury.

I stepped out my rocket made of tin,
Over a crater, *bang, bang,* what a din!
The moon is not what it seems to be
I've had enough now it's home time for me.

So I got in my rocket made of tin,
Now my journey home will begin.
Look out Mum, here I come!
Now my journey has been done.

Kacie Nash (9)
Westvale Primary School, Liverpool

Silly Astronauts

Twinkle, twinkle little star
How we wonder who we are
Astronauts wave hello to the stars
The stars wave back as they twinkle
Silly astronauts, silly astronauts, you don't have my treasure
Aliens come and say to them
Silly astronauts
Why are you here, you don't belong in space.

Eryn Jean McDonald (8)
Westvale Primary School, Liverpool

Spinny, Spinny Space

See the moon
Hear the tune
Space planets float just like a boat.

Aliens hang around the moon
In a big boom
Off they go.

One called Mo
One called Flo
One even has a
Very big toe!

Space is black
Just like my sack
I miss my Uncle Jack
But he'll be back.

Brooke Hewell (8)
Westvale Primary School, Liverpool

Unusual Space

Unusual space, unusual space
No need to race to unusual space,
The moon has eyes and eyelashes that rise
Unusual space, unusual space

Unusual stars, unusual stars
The unusual stars zoom as fast as the cars
Venus has a nose and hair that grows
Unusual stars, unusual stars

Unusual sun, unusual sun
The unusual sun is the shape of a bun
The sun has ears that are shaped like gears
Unusual sun, unusual sun.

Harry Farrell (9)
Westvale Primary School, Liverpool

Solo Planets

Space, space
Bright light
Asteroids boom
Rockets zoom
No delay
Fly all day
Come and play
In space one day
Come with me
See stars and Mars
Far away
Now I'll be on my way.

Joe Hart (8)
Westvale Primary School, Liverpool

Space Boots

S for star
P for planet
A for anti gravity
C for comet
E for Earth

B for boots
O for orbit
O for oxygen
T for travel
S for solar system.

Harvey James (8)
Westvale Primary School, Liverpool

Stars And Far

Trying to shine so far
A shining star glittering far
Running the star
Stars trying to find their way
Gravity travelling all the way
Learning their way to Venus
I like the stars, they are far
Trying to zoom and boom
Learning the way to Mars
Ra, ra, the stars shining.

Tegan Scott (8)
Westvale Primary School, Liverpool

All About Space

S tars are up in space
P lanets spinning round and round
A stronaut suit
C omet bursting down like lightning
E arth on different sides
S pace station getting ready for a rocket to land on the moon
H umans landing on the moon
I mpossible to land without a spacesuit
P ioneer 10 blasting off to the moon
S ee you soon!

Ryan Paul Wright (8)
Westvale Primary School, Liverpool

Dark Space

D ark is everywhere
A black hole is somewhere
R oaring rockets in the sky
K ey for the rocket

S pace is as dark as coal
P lanets are round and big
A liens are green as grass
C omets are bright
E arth is far away!

Joseph Bailey (9)
Westvale Primary School, Liverpool

Life In Space

Planets spin like a Catherine wheel
Aliens come out of flying saucers
Earth I flew past and it looked like grass and water
Comets fly past at the speed of light
Black hole disaster, what shall we do?
UFOs fly past
Galaxy I've flown around
Gravity was great
Yellow stars are beautiful.

Rhys Midgley (9)
Westvale Primary School, Liverpool

Space And All That Rubbish

Space, space, space like the night.
Stars, stars, stars so bright.
Astronauts, astronauts on Earth.
Travel to space, space, space.
Looking at planets, planets.
Rockets go boom.
And hear a boom.
All around space
Then time to go home.

Ross James Syms (9)
Westvale Primary School, Liverpool

Spacesuit

S paceships zooming around planets
P lanets floating like a plank of wood in a lake
A steroids exploding everywhere
C omets surrounding space
E arth still turning
S un melting space junk
U nit two and unit ten flying around
I ce planets
T he moon shining at night.

Conner Mark McGuire (9)
Westvale Primary School, Liverpool

Space Space

Space is by the stars that are close to Mars
The rockets land on the white sand

Stars are far, they're glittery and shiny
Looking like a diamond
I wish they were mine.

Space is cool, I love it.
If you go, you will know.

Marcus Ginley (9)
Westvale Primary School, Liverpool

Planets And Stars

Space, space full of stars
Venus, Jupiter and Mars.
Zero gravity makes you float
Just like water and a boat.
Planets floating in the sky
Look like crystals flying high.

Rhys Jacobs (9)
Westvale Primary School, Liverpool

Up In Space

S pinning planets in the dark
P luto is a planet
A stronauts getting ready for lift off
C omets sweeping towards the sun
E arth is where we live.

Madison-Leigh Murphy (8)
Westvale Primary School, Liverpool

YOUNG WRITERS INFORMATION

We hope you have enjoyed reading this book –
and that you will continue to in the coming years.

If you're a young writer who enjoys reading and
creative writing, or the parent of an enthusiastic poet or
story writer, do visit our website
www.youngwriters.co.uk. Here you will find free
competitions, workshops and games, as well as
recommended reads, a poetry glossary and our blog.

If you would like to order further copies of
this book, or any of our other titles give us
a call or visit **www.youngwriters.co.uk.**

Young Writers
Remus House
Coltsfoot Drive
Peterborough
PE2 9BF

(01733) 890066 / 898110
info@youngwriters.co.uk